THE ROBBER BARONS

THE
ROBBER BARONS

Saints or Sinners?

Edited by THOMAS B. BREWER
University of Toledo

ROBERT E. KRIEGER PUBLISHING COMPANY
HUNTINGTON, NEW YORK
1976

Cover illustration: "The Spiders and the Flies." Gould and Vanderbilt, as portrayed in a cartoon by Charles Kendrick. *(Boston Public Library)*

Original edition 1970
Reprint 1976

Printed and Published by
ROBERT E. KRIEGER PUBLISHING CO., INC.
645 NEW YORK AVENUE
HUNTINGTON, NEW YORK 11743

Library of Congress Cataloging in Publication Data
Brewer, Thomas B   comp.
     The robber barons.

     Reprint of the ed. published by Holt, Rinehart and
Winston, New York, in series: American problem studies.
     Bibliography: p.
     1. Capitalists and financiers--United States--
History--Addresses, essays, lectures. 2. United States--
Industries--History--Addresses, essays, lectures.
I. Title.
[HG181.B834 1976]   332'.0973   76-14793
ISBN 0-88275-429-7

Printed in the United States of America

CONTENTS

The cover of *Puck*, February 2, 1881. A cartoon by J. A. Wales depicting Gould and Vanderbilt carries the legend: "The Best Remedy. Uncle Sam: 'I guess a change of operators is wanted here.'"

INTRODUCTION

Concomitant with the economic growth of the late nineteenth century came many new problems for the United States, including a maldistribution of wealth, urban slums, farm distress, and the growing impersonalization of society. As economic change intensified and business expanded, the stewardship of the nation at that time passed from the politicians to a group of business leaders whose actions are still being evaluated and debated by historians. Some critics condemn these entrepreneurs as little more than greedy parasites on society, while others emphasize their creative ability as industrial statesmen. Although various shades of condemnation or praise lie between the two extremes, the majority of writers still adhere to the "robber baron" interpretation that the beliefs and policies of the post-Civil War businessman were detrimental to the nation.

The term robber baron, which came to be widely applied to the businessman of the latter 1900s, first appeared in the late 1860s in the writings of E. L. Godkin, editor of *The Nation*. Although used by Senator Carl Schurz of Missouri, the Grangers in the late 1870s, and the Greenbackers and Populists during the next two decades, "robber baron" became the historian's principal identifying concept after the appearance of Matthew Josephson's, *The Robber Barons: The Great American Capitalists, 1861–1901* (1934). However, present-day acceptance of the term and its implications has deep roots in the attitudes of post-Civil War Americans, and in order to focus sharply on the problem the student should understand the development of these attitudes and their effect on the writing of history.

The Gilded Age, so named by Mark Twain and Charles Dudley Warner, has been viewed over the years as a black-white period, mostly black. It is usually interpreted as an era of crass materialism, devoid of any redeeming characteristics. Much of this attitude may be traced to contemporaries, some of whom were serious reformers and others simply iconoclasts. They emphasized the venality of politics, the concentration of wealth, the crudities of taste, and the struggle of the masses.

The Progressive reformers of the early twentieth century reinforced such an appriasal of the period. In their efforts to bring about change, Progressive

1

writers offered the experiences of previous decades to prove their case. The work of Ida M. Tarbell, Lincoln Steffens, Thorstein Veblen, and a host of others strengthened the idea of a wasted generation. Two major historians writing in the 1920s, Vernon L. Parrington and Charles A. Beard, followed the Progressive tradition and did much to fix the interpretation for two generations.

This approach to the Gilded Age has prevailed down to our own day. Reevaluations have been few, and only recently have a growing number of scholars begun to emphasize the positive features of the late nineteenth century. Surely an era that produced E. L. Godkin, William Dean Howells, William James, Winslow Homer, Henry Hobson Richardson, Oliver Wendell Holmes, and Mark Twain cannot be entirely dismissed as decadent. Ironically, many of the leading contemporaries had helped shape the pessimistic view of the Gilded Age. The revisionist historians attempt to establish that politics contributed positively to the nation's growth, that the cultural level reached higher plateaus, and that education made great forward strides during this period. They claim that the failure to unravel the complexities of change, which was characterized by great energy and progress, has created a misunderstanding of the era.

All recent writers agree on one point: the big businessman stands as the symbol of the age. The product of corporate growth, he has been considered by many a threat to cherished ideas of individual freedom. As big business began to dominate the economy, the leaders of the giant enterprises assumed a central role in society. Before the Civil War the preeminence of politics and the small scale of commerce and industry obscured the role of businessmen, but the rapidity of postwar change thrust them into the limelight. In their new prominence, they appeared as both idols and devils, the creators of all that was good as well as all that was bad. In a word, they became the pivotal figures in society.

Many claim that the businessman ruthlessly abolished competition regardless of the consequences. Others counter that a definite code of ethics governed his behavior. Matthew Josephson, the best-known and most widely read proponent of the robber baron school of thought, in the first selection, holds that Henry Villard, one of the transporation leaders of the Pacific Northwest, sought a monopoly of commerce in that area. To gain that end, he worked out a scheme based on manipulation and fraud. Josephson pictures Villard as a man of mysterious moves, resembling an animal stealthily stalking his prey. The high point of his career was the organization of a syndicate, which entrusted Villard with huge sums of money for an unspecified purpose. The magnate soon unveiled his plan to seize control of the Northern Pacific Railroad and complete it to the West Coast. Villard's empire failed to endure, a point Josephson uses to indict the profit makers.

Thomas C. Cochran, perhaps the most influential revisionist historian of the last thirty years, directly challenges Josephson on Henry Villard's business role. Cochran attacks the premise of robber-baron writers that the entrepreneur operated amorally in an otherwise moral society and claims that all elements in society in fact clung to certain basic "cultural themes." Cochran emphasizes that the typical robber-baron approach to Villard, for example that of Josephson, overly dramatizes the story, particularly the "blind pool" incident. Cochran believes that the German-born Villard, rather than being a profit-seeking vulture, was a "relatively inexperienced entrepreneur" who lacked the ability to see his enterprise through a depression. He performed well in certain business roles, poorly in others. How was Villard's career part of the normal and repetitive process in big and small business? Did Villard "waste" capital or did his policies benefit long-run growth?

Pursuing the entreprenurial role in business methods to another industry, the name of John D. Rockefeller continually recurs in robber baron literature as the most ruthless tyrant in oil. One of the famous muckrakers in the Progressive period, Ida M. Tarbell, charges that Rockefeller wanted to eliminate all competition and create a monopoly. Granting John D.'s organizational talents, Tarbell accuses him of driving out smaller refiners by unscrupulous methods, sometimes by cutting the price or controlling railroad oil cars, but especially by using the rebate to gain a market advantage. Particularly unhappy about the Standard's use of dummy or subsidiary companies to acquire rivals, Tarbell questions the ethics more than the resulting efficiency of operations and condemns not only the "persuasion, intimidation, or force" applied but also the secrecy that surrounded Rockefeller's operations. She admits that some refiners received adequate compensation for their plants and that Rockefeller's attitudes characterized the entire industry, but she claims that the Standard Oil Company applied unethical methods to an extent unknown before that time.

Ralph W. and Muriel Hidy think that there was little difference between the Standard Oil managers' views of competition and those of most of their contemporaries. Moreover, although the Standard Oil men attempted to create a monopoly, they were unable to achieve this goal by the 1880s. The Hidys maintain, however, that in the expansionist period of the 1870s, the one described by Tarbell, the company paid fair prices to refiners who sold out, preferring this approach to fighting. They do not deny the use of tactics described by Tarbell or the attempts at secrecy; rather, they emphasize, as the key to Standard Oil's success, the long-range planning and development of an efficient management team controlling centralized policy decisions. Regardless of the methods used, Rockefeller "brought a measure of order to a formerly confused industry." Which is more important to long-term growth, ethics or efficiency? Is the assertion that the men of Standard used tactics employed by others a valid one? Or is it mere rationalization? What is the proper relationship between ethics and competition?

Another question concerns the general climate of opinion. Did the businessman have a philosophy by which he justified not only his business methods but his stewardship of society? It is usually said that he did: the doctrine of Social Darwinism. Popularized by the Englishman Herbert Spencer, the philosophy emphasized a natural order in society determined by the survival of the fittest. Richard Hofstadter claims that Spencer's writing enjoyed great vogue in the United States and strongly influenced not only the entrepreneur's approach to society, but other areas of intellectual activity as well. He concludes that "it symbolized the harmony of the new science with the outlook of a business civilization."

Irvin G. Wyllie challenges Hofstadter's conclusions and expresses strong reservations as to Social Darwinism's pervasive influence on the captains of industry. Wyllie claims that most intellectual historians have exaggerated the impact of this philosophy, and he singles out Hofstadter for special attention. He points out that Hofstadter used only four businessmen to prove his case, and Wyllie casts doubt on their statements. He claims that the moguls used Social Darwinism to defend their actions only on rare occasions. They relied more on pre-Darwinian religious and economic ideas. These conflicting interpretations suggest the difficulties in assessing historical data, even after long and thoughtful research.

One of the symbols of the mogul's position in society was his mode of living, which often included palatial mansions and gold-trimmed carriages. Viewing this as conspicuous waste and a manifestation of the increasing inequality of wealth, Thorstein Veblen unleashed his sardonic wit on the "leisure class," which roughly consisted of the robber barons. Veblen believed that edifices, household interiors, and even spoons should be designed for utility and that any ornamentation reflected the penchant for conspicuous waste. Always present in his colorful descriptions of this waste is the theme of its corrupting effect on human values.

Edward Chase Kirkland opposes Veblen's view of conspicuous living as overgeneralized and too simplistic. Choosing the "big house" as an example, Kirkland holds that many factors accounted for the existence of mansions, among them the influence of architects, reaction to poor backgrounds, and pressure from wives. Noting the various attacks on the big house by contemporaries in the Gilded Age, Kirkland finds it difficult to reject the apology that such homes employed labor and encouraged the arts. Does Kirkland offer an adequate defense of the big house as it reflected conspicuous living? Or is Veblen more to the point in his position that such standards corrupted human values? Did the big businessman have the right to spend his own money in any way he saw fit? Or should he have demonstrated more concern with alternative uses for his wealth?

As the mogul looked at the world around him, how did he view the men who worked to produce his great affluence? Henry David represents the traditional Progressive interpretation of the period when he ascribes the workingman's problems to the growth of the large corporation, with its resulting impersonalization of labor-management relations. As the inequalities in wealth steadily increased, the captains of industry demonstrated a callousness toward the worker and saw him simply as a commodity to be purchased at the lowest price. Labor's attempts to relieve its sufferings were defeated by a corrupt political system controlled by business interests. Although David agrees that not all workers received inhuman treatment, he concludes that the labor violence of the era was caused by real grievances.

Herbert Gutman criticizes the traditional approach to labor relations in the Gilded Age as too generalized, particularly the notion that the new power structure immediately destroyed long-established social ideas. His case against stereotyping labor is based on the differences in social attitudes existing in large urban areas and in small industrial towns. Granting that impersonal relationships characterized large cities, thereby allowing the businessman to manipulate the laborer, Gutman claims that smaller communities held more closely to the older human values. The social structure thus limited the employer's freedom of action, and in order to enforce decisions, such as wage cuts, he often had to call for outside assistance. The personal involvement of lawyers, professional people, newspaper editors, and local politicians with the working class increased the difficulty of business exploitation of the laborer.

In addition to the influence, moral or amoral, of the businessman on philosophy, life style, and the working class, his critics often cite the corrupting nature of his political activities. He is usually portrayed, as in the selection by Gustavus Myers, as ruthlessly manipulating legislative bodies, primarily through bribery. Myers describes the activities of the "Pacific Quartet"—Collis Huntington, Leland Stanford, Mark Hopkins, and Charles Crocker—within a Marxist frame of reference. In this black-white portrayal, the Central Pacific–Southern Pacific magnates emerge as villains operating against a weak-willed, helpless Congress. Their activities are seen to result in the milking of public treasuries and the degrading of the American political system.

But was the situation as clearcut as Myers claims? David J. Rothman, the leading authority on the structure and policies of the Senate during the Gilded Age, thinks not. Railroads possessed little capital and did not savor the idea of spending it to influence legislation. Rothman does not deny that the railroad interests, and many other pressure groups for that matter, attempted to secure favorable laws, but he insists on a distinction between bribery and the legitimate activities of lobbyists. He specifically cites Huntington's activities in Washington, which the California magnate claimed were to insure a "full and sympathetic congressional hearing." Even with the granting of loans and passes, no senator could be counted on to support pet projects. Rothman concludes that business interests did not control the Senate, and the period simply represents the beginning of the modern system of lobbying. Given the shortage of capital for railroads and the public's agreement on their necessity, were the moguls right in expecting government aid? Was the result worth the investment? Is lobbying a legitimate form of influencing legislation? Did railroad managers behave differently from other interest groups? Although they were dominant figures in society, were they always successful in the use of power?

To this point, the writers present conflicting views. But is there a middle ground? Fritz Redlich claims that the Gilded Age mogul was dynamic and creative, but also destructive. His approach, often called consensus history, is widely accepted by historians trained in the 1950s and early 1960s, but rejected by a large portion of those who matured in the 1940s or earlier and by those now beginning their careers who are labeled "New Left" historians.

Redlich, writing in the 1950s, maintains that every creative act contains the seeds of destruction for something else; therefore the robber baron, with his reliance on rugged individualism, doomed himself as a fixture in society not because of his ruthlessness but because of his achievements. Redlich also discusses the businessman's "avoidable destructiveness," which was not related to creativity, and offers an explanation based on generation theory. Claiming that while creative-destructive patterns have always characterized business, Redlich shows that they did not crystallize until the late nineteenth century, when the mogul's accumulation of power began to threaten the institutional fabric of society and resulted in the rise of other power groups which weakened his position.

The Gilded Age captain of industry played many roles in society. Besides shaping the business climate, he profoundly influenced—or was believed to have influenced—the way men thought, the cultural life of the nation, and its political institutions. The controversy surrounding these roles continues to characterize writing on late-nineteenth-century entrepreneurs. Evaluating them is a real challenge to the student attempting to understand one of the more complex problems in American history—and a challenge to those striving for the patience and open-mindedness that the search for objectivity demands.

In the reprinted selections footnotes appearing in the original sources have in general been omitted unless they contribute to the argument or better understanding of the selection.

MATTHEW JOSEPHSON (b. 1899) is the most widely quoted writer on the captains of industry. His book on the Gilded Age businessman, from which this selection is taken, made the term robber baron part of the language. Josephson, a journalist, was strongly influenced in his thinking by the depression conditions of the 1930s and the writings of Gustavus Myers. Although he has written several other books, including *The Politicos, 1865–1896* (1938) and *Edison: A Biography* (1959), none has had as much impact as *The Robber Barons.* Josephson accuses Henry Villard, a Gilded Age railroad leader, of attempting to monopolize transportation in the Northwest by applying unethical, secret, and illegal tactics to crush his would-be competitors.*

Matthew Josephson

The Unethical Maneuverings
of Henry Villard

A man of wide culture (compared to our indigenous economic leaders), of varied adventure and high imagination, Henry Villard (né Heinrich Hilgard) had come from Bavaria to the United States in 1853 at the age of nineteen, and soon proceeded as far west as Colorado. After working as a traveling journalist for German newspapers, then as a war correspondent for Greeley's *Tribune,* Villard had made himself useful in the immigration service of Jay Cooke. Quick-witted, magnetic and eloquent, Villard seemed to win successes with but the least exertion; he attracted friends and followers everywhere. In 1871 he revisited his native country. The knowledge of railroad affairs he had gathered brought

him eventually an appointment as financial agent for the groups of defrauded German bondholders. Thus, having returned to the United States, in 1874 he toured Oregon to examine the affairs of the Oregon steamship lines and railways in the interests of the foreign investors.

Introduced to the transportation business on the Pacific Coast, all he learned determined Villard to acquire and unite these various properties, part of which had fallen from the hands of Cooke and as to whose value the foreign creditors were permanently disillusioned.

He was dazzled by the discovery of a beautiful frontier province, giant forests, mineral deposits, rich farm lands in the broad Oregon valleys. His memoirs, written in the Victorian manner in the third person, say:

What he saw of the scenery of Oregon on the way to Portland in the California, Yoncalla and Willamette valleys filled him with enthusiasm. . . . His lengthy printed report to the committee contained favorable accounts of his impressions of western Oregon, and expressed his belief in the promising future of the country and consequently in the certain improvement in the prospects of the bondholders. The greatest assurance of this lay in increase of population. . . .

He saw that "the vast region drained by the Columbia and its tributaries formed a very empire in its extent." Deep into this inland empire the ships proceeded up the long Columbia and Snake rivers. Its material development was absolutely dependent, he felt, "upon the present and future transportation facilities within its limits." At this time the western limit of the Northern Pacific Railroad lay only at Bismarck, on the Missouri River.

According to one account given in Barron's diary by W. H. Starbuck, a colleague of Villard's, an account graphic enough though perhaps faulty in its recollection of details, Villard, while studying and occupying himself with the shipping business on the Northwest Coast, made inquiries concerning the Columbia River Line ships. These were owned by the Oregon Steam Navigation Company, and Villard "unexpectedly found that they were earning handsomely, but could be bought for three million dollars." Thereupon he acquired from the owners a four months' option for $100,000, which he and his associates bestirred themselves to raise, and which permitted the purchase of a majority stock control in these shipping properties.

Villard went to New York, *incorporated his option* under the name of the "Oregon Railway and Navigation Company" with 60,000 shares of capital stock, not paid. He then went to the Farmers' Loan & Trust Company of New York, and by a wonderful piece of legerdemain executed a mortgage against the properties to be acquired. He was able to use the proceeds, as well as the funds from further bond sales, to purchase in accordance with the terms of his option control of the steamship companies of Oregon. Thus with a single stroke (like so many of his brilliant contemporaries) he had actual possession of a property which was soon valued at $10,000,000. "Then came the boom of 1879 and soon Villard and I were rolling in money," concludes Starbuck's account.

Shortly afterward, Villard took steps to unite certain other shipping companies of the Pacific Coast and river trade with his own holding company. To these were added various allied short railroads, already constructed in the region, including a line running up the Columbia Valley, and soon the daring Villard was issuing glowing statements to the speculative public of Wall Street, according to Henry Clews's account—"a carefully prepared report showing immense and unprecedented earnings." The stock of Oregon Railway & Navigation which Villard confesses "five months before had been given as a bonus" to certain Wall Street leaders, rose to a price of 95. This was simply due, as his autobiography tells us, to the fact that

net earnings of the two constituent . . . companies were sufficiently large to warrant the payment of bond interest and eight per cent dividends on the stock, payment at which rate had already been commenced. This astonishing increase naturally raised Mr. Villard to a still more commanding position in Wall Street.

We see here a style of campaign which has become familiar to a modern generation. Stock issues flowed rapidly and dividends seemed to be paid almost as soon as the capital was raised, without the least delay for use of the capital. Soon, against visible assets estimated at $3,500,000 (fully mortgaged) some $18,000,000 in stock was issued and placed on the market. With the aid of the Wall Street pool leader, Woerishoffer, Villard, as Henry Clews relates, "had the stock bulled to 200." Here the older broker in his own memoirs comments, with unkindness or with envy—it is hard to tell—"as a stock waterer Villard had probably no superior in that important department of railway management."

Having "glory and cash" aplenty and standing high in Wall Street, Villard now for two years pursued a brilliantly conceived campaign to consolidate his gains and fix his grip on the "narrows" of the Northwestern arteries of trade. First, he and his group began pre-empting a route along the Columbia River, by "laying down a cheap narrow gauge road." It was an expensive process; the line would be useless in a few years and would have to be torn up; but thereafter, at least, no other adventuring knight of railroads could move down the south bank of the Columbia River, the only side on which railroad tracks could be laid.

He and his men then secretly scoured the huge region, spying out the valleys and mountain passes and river banks that must be possessed. Villard, with imagination aflame, had a tremendous plan afoot which envisaged nothing less than seizure of all the possible routes and approaches to the Pacific Ocean in the Oregon and Washington country, thus blocking the line of march of the second transcontinental railroad, the Northern Pacific.

One stroke follows another, as Villard moves among the rival railroad groups, mysteriously skirmishing for vital posi-

tions, as in a game with pawns and mock artillery. Now he seizes the confluence of the Columbia and the Snake River, destined, as his engineers showed him, to be the gateway to the Pacific Northwest; now he occupies the northern approaches to the Columbia River Valley in Washington, "the most strategic positions and richest agricultural areas." It was, as his agent in the field reported to him, "a country well worth fighting for," since it prevented the forging of a link of some 200 miles by the Northern Pacific between Lake Pend Oreille and the head of navigation on the Columbia.

In the meantime, he conducted campaigns to hamper the enemy's construction, setting the rival towns against each other, lobbying in the state capitols, or now shifting his movements with almost comic haste when he learned that the opponent was circumventing him by moving up another valley.

"Let me drop everything else," his lieutenant Thielsen reports, "and let me get our road up Union Flat . . . and some distance over into the Clearwater country located, with right of way secured, and even commence work on it before the other party can make preparations or is aware of what we are doing."

Huntington understood the process quite clearly. He himself had railway interests in Oregon, and he set up a cry of alarm, "threatened and remonstrated with the Union Pacific people," so strongly that Gould and Dillon, who had been conniving passively with Villard, were detached as allies. But the progress of Villard could no longer be stopped.

Having seized the mountain passes and valleys, Villard relates how he also gathered valuable coal deposits to unite with his transportation business. Thus fortified, having the Northern Pacific well bottled and clashing with it at every point, he tried to negotiate an accord for dividing the traffic. After some resistance the hostile Northern Pacific men in October, 1880, signed a presumably friendly prorating agreement with the Villard roads and ships, allowing passage of freight and travelers from one line to the other. But by this means the enemy was only treacherously biding his time. His intention was to raise great sums of money in order to crush Villard in Washington and also Jim Hill, whose Manitoba in the Dakotas paralleled his line.

But in November, 1880, Villard learned of the secret sale by Northern Pacific of $40,000,000 of its first mortgage bonds to a powerful banking syndicate headed by Drexel, Morgan & Co., August Belmont and others. Villard relates: "The transaction, then unparalleled in its magnitude, assured to the company $36,000,000 of money, which was then generally assumed to be sufficient for the completion and equipment of the entire main line." Thus within a month the Northern Pacific was in a position to advance against him and his "entire defensive position was entirely changed."

The case was desperate. Should the Northern Pacific, crossing Idaho, reach the Columbia River, then certainly the market value of Villard's whole pyramid of sprawling little rail and ship lines would crumble away overnight. Villard therefore resolved upon measures as desperate as his circumstances warranted. He hurried to New York and formed the famous "blind pool" of 1881 which for its Napoleonic boldness of conception long represented a peak in the high finance of the epoch.

All through 1880 Villard had been making secret purchases of Northern Pacific stock. But now he called together all the moneyed persons who had been following him in his exploits and who

heartily admired him because wherever he went almost instantly securities bloomed and flowered with rich dividends. Ernestly and confidentially he addressed a gathering of about fifty persons in his office asking them to subscribe to a "syndicate" in the sum of $8,000,000. The purpose of the syndicate, or pool, he did not divulge in his confidential circulars save to a very few trusted associates such as George Pullman and the German plunger, Woerishoffer. Beside himself with emotion, with the strange eloquence he possessed in such emergencies, he indicated to his followers that the undertaking had such tremendous potentialities for profit and power that one dared not speak of it. The very mystery of the affair caused a rush of subscriptions. Villard's office in New York was crowded with speculators, and the subscriptions soon commanded a premium of from 25 to 40 per cent.

In the summer of 1881 Villard called another meeting of the subscribers to reveal his plans for buying the Northern Pacific, and they now agreed to subscribe $12,000,000 more to the formation of a new corporation, the "Oregon & Transcontinental Company," a holding company which at once issued $30,000,000 of stock among the subscribers for the $20,000,000 of cash paid in. Finally in September, 1881, after sensational maneuvers in the market, control of the long railroad passed to Villard. He then joined it with his Pacific Coast properties under the new holding company, which had the widest powers to "construct for the others" as usual, to merge the others, to engage in mining, shipping, land-jobbing, town-building, or to seize every possible natural site or position of advantage. Nothing seemed to have been overlooked in the charter.

Thousands of men now labored in the

mountains to finish the main line of the Northern Pacific. No sooner was he in full charge of the system than Villard, in 1881, declared a dividend of 11 $\frac{1}{10}$ per cent to its stockholders "against improvements made from earnings," a gesture typical of him. At the same time the new president made a tremendous effort to populate his railroad barony. He filled the entire world with his pictures, stereopticon slides and "literature" illustrating the Eden-like Northwestern territories. Hundreds of his immigration agents spread their dragnet throughout Europe and England, hauling the peasants from Germany and Sweden in by the thousands to Oregon and the Columbia Basin; de-populating sometimes whole villages in Russia. These vast migrations, which brought, in one instance a train of 6,000 wagons across the Rockies, were inspired of course by an excessive enthusiasm. In the case of the Scandinavians especially, agents were reported to have deceived the peasant "by painting too bright a picture of the future awaiting him in the new land."

When the road was completed Villard, who had a passion for publicity and for eye-filling gestures, advertised the business to the whole world by making a record-breaking passage across the continent "on business." Through the courtesy of other railroad officials he was able to arrange for a special train running through without stopping except for a change of locomotives every 200 miles. The whole Western public watched his progress and cheered him on, he recalls with pride, as he descended at Portland in less than half the regular time, the fastest trip ever made.

The completion of the main line to the Pacific in 1883, was attended with a series of celebrations through which Henry Villard moved like a great prince occupy-ing the whole stage. His private train passed in a triumphal procession through the newly made towns along the way. In his car his guests of honor were President Arthur, General Grant, Secretary Evarts and other cabinet members, ambassadors such as Viscount James Bryce, Congressmen, governors; newspaper reporters, soldiers and Indians filled four special trains. In the incidental entertainments, exhibitions of track-laying were held, followed by artillery salutes, speech-making and the music of brass bands. Sitting Bull was brought from captivity for one occasion. And for the final festival of the Golden Spike, on September 8, 1883, the Crow Head tribe and their chief appeared and in a symbolic gesture formally ceded their hunting grounds to the big chief of the Northern Pacific, who described the historic affairs of the Golden Spike in his memoirs:

A thousand feet of track had been left unfinished in order to give the guests a demonstration of the rapidity with which the rails were put down. This having been done, amidst the roar of artillery, the strains of military music, and wild cheering Mr. Villard hammered down the "last spike."

The affair left an unforgettable impression upon Bryce who, pondering upon the character of the American institutions, wrote shortly afterward in his "American Commonwealth":

. . . These railway kings are among the greatest men, perhaps I may say the greatest men, in America. . . . They have power, more power—that is, more opportunity of making their will prevail—than perhaps any one in political life, except the President and the Speaker who, after all hold theirs only for four years and two years, while the railroad monarch may keep his for life.

Yet in this case the king was not fated to rule for long. At the very time that Henry

Villard stood sunning himself in glory, doffing his hat and bowing to the madly cheering throng, at this moment when six houses were being torn down in Madison Avenue, New York, to make way for the palace of the railroad "magnate," his spirits were heavy and he felt himself in utmost danger. Like a deadly disease the secret deficit of his whole enterprise was increasing, eating into the core of the thing.

In demeanor and in word he dared not show his great trouble, standing as before an abyss and with a mask of composure. But three months before the festive completion of the road private report from his officers had showed the cost of construction through grievous miscalculation to have exceeded the original estimates by $14,000,000, which, added to an existing deficit of $5,500,000, made it impossible even for such a magician as he to escape disaster. Magician though he was and elected by himself to develop a Northwestern empire, Henry Villard apparently knew little enough about railroad-building. For the ceremony of the Golden Spike he had to borrow a good locomotive from Jim Hill, according to gossip retold long afterward in Barron's journals. In all his work there had been a woeful haste and waste, a costly series of errors and lootings by the inside "construction company," typical of much of the hurly-burly empire-building of the day.

Here is the testimony of an able railroad chief at the time. James Hill, in intramural correspondence with his old fellow conspirator, Lord Mount Stephen, spoke of the "long stretch of entirely worthless country on the other Pacific roads" (Union and Northern Pacific); of their bad grades and high interest charges, winding up: "I feel . . . that they are not really competitors," that is, with an honestly capitalized well-constructed

road. He added also in a letter to Charles Elliot Perkins, head of the friendly Burlington, what he thought particularly of Villard's "developments":

The lines are located in a good country, some of it rich, and producing a large tonnage; but the capitalization is far ahead of what it should be for what there is to show, and the selection of the routes and grades is abominable. Practically it would have to be built over.

Villard now realized that all his confident statements to his associates and followers would be discredited. His securities would decline. Moreover, blows seemed to fall upon him every day from unexpected quarters. Small privateers who pounced upon franchises or built short rail lines in his territory practiced blackmail upon him. In Washington his mighty adversaries, Gould and Huntington, lobbied to bring about the forfeiture of the Northern Pacific's land grant, causing him to reply in outbursts of indignation—though he himself had used the same tactics yesterday when trying to capture the road from its previous owners. Finally, at this evil hour the pressure of Hill's competitive strokes was too much. The Manitoba, the future Great Northern, crept steadily through Villard's domain, preempting the business at lower rates, while Hill boasted privately that he meant for the moment to keep his tariffs down in certain regions so that "opposition enterprises must be bankrupt." Hill could show on a piece of paper what it cost exactly to haul a loaded car over the grades of the Northern Pacific and what it would cost over his own line. According to Pyle, his intensely admiring biographer:

Mr. Hill let Mr. Villard have his fill of glory; did not sulk or protest when he became the talk of two continents; took care not to offend his amour propre, and thus succeeded very well in maintaining a working understanding by which the Manitoba Company was permitted to go its way in peace. . . .

The Northern Pacific . . . most powerful concern in the Pacific Northwest [its steamships having eliminated river competition] . . . had no terrors for Mr. Hill. He knew its financial condition, notwithstanding the . . . apparent plethora of cash. Better yet he knew its operating condition. . . . He was in no hurry or fret, because he knew that every day reduced the power of the Northern Pacific to carry its own burdens. . . .

Now in his extremity began the grim pursuit of credit for Villard, over whom a shadow hung. He issued $20,000,000 more in mortgage bonds with ill success. His securities continued to sink. As his grip weakened his former associates stabbed at him from behind with the stiletto, according to the traditional ethics of their trade in Wall Street. As he tottered they pushed hard. His recollections are painful here:

> Mr. Villard learned then the lesson taught him so often in Wall Street, that the throng of people which follows with alacrity the man who leads them to profits, will desert him just as quickly when he ceases to be a money-maker for them. He soon found that many of his most trusted friends, who formerly visited his offices regularly, had sold out their holdings and stayed away. He even discovered downright treachery among his confidential advisers, two of the Oregon and Transcontinental directors using their private knowledge of the condition of the company for enormous "short" sales of its shares.

Collapse came swiftly on the heels of his triumph. In January, 1884, owning that "neither he nor the Oregon & Transcontinental could be saved," Villard resigned from all his united enterprises, which sank toward the gulf of bankruptcy together amid the tremendous clamor of investors who had been brought to ruin, a scandal as sensational as anything which Jay Gould had ever evoked. Among promoters of "large railway combination," Villard was long the butt of public anger and the popular press pointed bitterly to the luxurious mansion on Madison Avenue in which he still continued to live after his reverses. Here Villard dwelt amid so much costly and empty splendor because he had "no other city home" and "for reasons of economy," while pondering new magic for the future. Though his memory was hated in the Northwest country, where "the specter of monopoly haunted the settlers," he had more or less knowingly, and after his own happy-go-lucky fashion, hastened the process of centralization taking place in the industrial life of America.

THOMAS C. COCHRAN (b. 1902), professor of history at the University of Pennsylvania, for a quarter of a century has been one of the leaders in what is called "entrepreneurial" history, which focuses on the businessman in his historical setting. His best-known work, written with William Miller, is *The Age of Enterprise: A Social History of Industrial America* (1942). His other books include *History of the Pabst Brewing Company* (1948), *Railroad Leaders, 1845–1890* (1953), *The American Business System 1900–1955* (1957), and *The Puerto Rican Businessman* (1959). In this selection Cochran challenges Josephson's interpretation of Henry Villard and maintains that the late-nineteenth-century businessman should be evaluated within his own cultural frame of reference and not by mid-twentieth-century standards. He concludes that the only valid approach to the study of entrepreneurship is to apply social science methodology to comparative cultural studies and to proceed from the particular to the general. Does Cochran offer an effective alternative to Josephson's thesis?*

Thomas C. Cochran

Villard: The Positive Side

Between business history, which has concentrated attention upon the administration of the firm, and general social or economic history, which has frequently omitted business processes altogether, there is a broad, vacant area. In this twilight zone lie the relations of business leaders with similar men in other firms, the interactions of businessmen with society as a whole, and the economic effects of business decisions. Scholars viewing this area have seen such a host of related problems that a group composed of representatives from some of the East Coast universities has given the study a special name: entrepreneurial history. In defining this field, the term entrepreneur has not been restricted to the conventional American textbook meaning of one who risks capital in enterprise. Rather, the older French definitions of Cantillon and Say have been re-expressed in broader language to make entrepreneur roughly equivalent to business executive. In the research of the group, the function of entrepreneurship, or business leadership, is conceived as operating in a broad socio-economic setting. . . .

An analysis of the period in which

*From Thomas C. Cochran, "The Legend of the Robber Barons," *Pennsylvania Magazine of History and Biography,* LXXIV (1950), pp. 307, 309–316. Footnotes omitted.

many American historians have discussed the businessman, the age of the "robber barons," will illustrate the reinterpretation that may come from entrepreneurial history. The "robber barons" are usually selected from among the railroad, industrial, and financial leaders of the period from about 1865 to 1900, and more often than not are the only businessmen who appear in college textbooks covering this period. According to the present historical mythology, they are seen as "bad" or unusually grasping and unscrupulous types in our culture against the background of a "good" public. The interest in discussing them is to illustrate business malpractices, and, presumably, to convey moralistic warnings against such activities, rather than to understand the business process in society.

In distinction to this pathological approach, the entrepreneurial historian is interested in the culture patterns and social structures which have produced these assumed types, and in whether or not the types have been correctly delineated. In pursuing such a study, the first thing is to decide what some of the major cultural themes were that guided or sanctioned the roles of these men. I think we can pick out three about which there will be little controversy: the concept of the autonomous economy that was self-adjusting; the idea that progress came through competition and the survival of the fittest; and the belief that profit or material gain was the only reliable incentive for action. These themes operated throughout the society as a whole. The truckman delivering dirt for railroad construction was as much motivated by profit and as firm a believer in these themes as was the "robber baron" who was building the road. The dissident element in the society, those who denied the value of these major themes, seem during these years to have been a relatively small, or at least unin-

fluential, portion of the population. Therefore, if value judgments are to be formed, they should be applied to this type of society or culture. It is rather futile to assert that the culture would have been all right if it were not for the kind of people and activities that resulted directly from its major themes.

If one accepts the additional and continuing American theme that material growth is a reliable index of progress, and its usual corollary that rapid progress is desirable, one question that may be asked of the culture as a whole is whether such progress could have taken place faster if other beliefs had prevailed. Since it is impossible to conceive deductively what the United States would have been like if built up on some other system, such a decision requires the establishment of a comparative standard. But if recourse is had to the history of another nation in order to observe the application of different cultural patterns to economic development, none seems like the United States to offer satisfying parallels. It is interesting, however, to note that in one of the somewhat similar economic situations, that of Australia, where railroads and frontier development went on through more state enterprise, about the same things were complained of that commentators here in the United States blamed upon private enterprise. In other words, a number of the difficulties seem to have been inherent in the rapid development of a pioneer area rather than in the particular means by which the development went on.

Avoiding, therefore, such unanswerable questions, and concentrating on a better understanding of the operation of American culture, let us examine the historical legend of the "robber baron" by analyzing the "case history" of Henry Villard. Villard is an interesting "robber baron" because he was brought up outside the American culture in a German bureau-

cratic or official family. His father was
a German lawyer and judge, who ultimately became a member of the Supreme
Court of the Kingdom of Bavaria. Villard,
after attendance at three European universities, decided to come to the United
States to try his fortune. Supported to
some extent by family money, he entered
journalism and built himself a successful
career as a correspondent for European
and American newspapers. The Civil
War, particularly, gave prestige to young
Villard. He was able to interview Lincoln
and to offer many interesting and pene-
trating views of contemporary events. In
the early seventies he went back to Germany, and through his family connections came to know the chief financial
men of Frankfort and Munich. These
contacts led to his being sent over as a
representative of German bondholders in
the Oregon railroad and steamship enterprises that had fallen into difficulties
during the depression following the panic
of 1873.

It is interesting that when Villard was
placed in the position of having to make
judgments regarding what should be done
on the unfinished Oregon and California
Railroad and in regard to the river navigation projects, he readily assumed the
entrepreneurial role in just about the
same form as men who had been brought
up in business. In other words, the entrepreneurial role seems to have been so
much a part of the cultural pattern of
America, and possibly of middle class
Germany, at this time, that there was no
great gulf between the attitude of the
professional intellectual or journalist
and that of the businessman. Villard
identified himself quickly with the development of the Oregon area, and, instead
of advising liquidation and withdrawal
for his German clients, he counseled
rather the investment of still more cap-

ital in order to complete the enterprises.
In this way his essential role was that of
attracting foreign capital to a frontier
development. It is not clear that he was
ever deeply interested in problems of
technology and management—that is, in
just how the capital was applied for productive purposes; rather, he became a
public relations man for the area, and an
over-all or general entrepreneurial super-
visor of where the capital should be allo-
cated.

One factor of great importance in the
Villard story is that he started new activities at just about the bottom of the deep
depression that lasted from 1873 to 1879,
and his ventures from then on, or at least
from 1877 on, were first on a gradually
rising market, and finally, from 1879 to
1882, on a market that boomed.

Villard saw quickly that the Northern
Pacific Railroad, which was being built
across the country from Duluth and St.
Paul, would have to make, or at least
should make, an agreement to connect
with whatever road occupied the Columbia River valley. With this long-range
plan in mind, he secured foreign and
domestic help for the building of the
Oregon Railroad and Navigation Company up the Columbia, at a time when
Northern Pacific construction was moving
very slowly into eastern Montana.

It is from this point on that the most
interesting differences occur between the
dramatic "robber baron" explanation of
Villard's activities and the more sober and
socially complex explanation offered by
entrepreneurial history. The "robber
baron" story is, that as Villard found the
Northern Pacific management nearing
the Columbia valley but unwilling to
agree to make use of his facilities—that
is, threatening to build either a parallel
line or to cross the Cascade Mountains
to Tacoma and Seattle—he decided that

he must get control of the Northern Pacific. So great was his prestige for successful operation by this time that he had the boldness to ask a group of his friends in Wall Street to put up $8,000,000 for some project that he would not reveal to them. And, as the story went, he had no difficulty in more than raising the first payment requested for this "blind pool," money which he used secretly to buy control of the Northern Pacific Railroad. The "robber baron" analogy is, of course, obvious and exciting. The "robber baron," Villard, seizes control of a strategic pass and then exacts tribute from the railroad that represents a great, nationally subsidized enterprise. Villard's blind pool has all of the trappings of high drama and shady financial dealings. The "robber baron" story then goes on to assert that Villard robbed the Northern Pacific and his other properties in the course of construction in such a way so that by 1883 they were bankrupt, while he himself had become very rich.

As usual, the actual story is not so dramatic. What appears to have happened is, that when the Northern Pacific secured Drexel Morgan financing in the latter part of the year 1880, and the Drexel Morgan-Winslow Lanier syndicate learned that Frederick Billings, the president of Northern Pacific, was planning to build duplicate facilities to the coast without regard to the already existing Oregon Railroad and Navigation Company, they became worried over the economic loss involved in constructing nearly parallel lines. The bankers, not sharing in the loyalties to individual companies that presidents and other officers almost inevitably develop, could see no reason why Northern Pacific and O.R. & N. could not get together in one co-operating line. But some of the officers of Northern Pacific, particularly Billings, regarded the

railroad as their greatest life work; they felt that to compromise and make the final road a joint venture between the "upstart" Villard and the great Northern Pacific enterprise was a personal defeat. Whereupon Morgan, at least, decided that the only way of bringing about a compromise and preventing unnecessary construction was to establish a common control for the two companies. Since Villard, who had, from the financial standpoint, acquitted himself well as receiver for Kansas Pacific, was now anxious to get this joint control, and assured Morgan that he independently had the resources to do so, the syndicate gave him their blessings, and even offered him their help. The "blind pool" was, therefore, chiefly a product of Villard's love of drama, of doing things in a spectacular fashion. Had he been willing to forgo these dramatic frills, control could quietly have been bought through the syndicate over about the same period. Of course, it cannot be overlooked that successfully doing the job himself gave Villard great personal prestige in Wall Street.

The difficulties from 1881 on to the completion of the road in 1883 seem to have been to some extent inevitable, and to some extent to have resulted from the usual overoptimism of American promoters. Villard formed a holding company, called the Oregon and Transcontinental Company, which was to own stocks in his various enterprises, make the construction contracts, and generally conduct the building which would weld Northern Pacific and O.R. & N. into one system. Undoubtedly, the Oregon and Transcontinental Company stock was a source of large profit for Villard; in fact, it seems probable that all the money Villard made in connection with these enterprises came from floating, buying, and selling the securities in Wall Street. It may be that Villard profited from the construction contracts, but there is no clear evidence of this, and it is quite possible, by analogy to similar situations, that the profits of construction went largely to local contractors in the West. At all events, the major difficulty was a lack of sufficient traffic to warrant the high construction cost of building railroads through the Rockies and the Oregon coastal regions. The completion of the through-line in August of 1883 was almost simultaneous with the beginning of a steady recession in general business that ended in a crisis the following March. As a result, the difficulties that the system would have experienced in paying returns under any circumstances were accentuated. When the companies were not able to pay dividends and their securities declined, Villard, temporarily losing the confidence of the banking syndicate, was forced to retire from the control of the various enterprises.

One way, therefore, of looking at this whole story is that Villard, a relatively inexperienced entrepreneur, took hold of a series of frontier developments at the bottom of the business cycle, carried them along through his connections and personal enthusiasm during the rise of the cycle, completed them just at the peak of the boom, and was then unable to steer them through the ensuing depression. Viewed from this angle, the whole development was a normal and repetitive one in both big and small business. The general history of even a small retail store or factory enterprise was often just about the same; if the enterprise started at a favorable time in the business cycle, it could last until a major depression. Then, unless it has had farsighted and unusually able management, or had been lucky in making more profit than was possible for

most young enterprises, it lapsed into bankruptcy and had to be reorganized with the injection of new capital. The roles that Villard played extremely well were those of a mobilizer of capital resources for pioneer investments, and effective public relations for the development of an area. The roles that he played poorly were those of an expert railroad builder and conservative business forecaster.

What do entrepreneurial historians expect to gain from such a study? In the first place, the study of outstanding examples such as that of Villard may be instructive for the study of the normal practices and operations of business. A detailed study of the Villard enterprises will show more exactly the nature of such practices as the strategic type of entrepreneurship that went into railroad building. The seizing of the transportation route down the Columbia River is merely a dramatic example of the general type of planning done by all western railroad builders. The strategic occupation of territory was like a great game of chess. Each leading entrepreneur had to guess where his rivals were likely to build next, how he could forestall their entrance into an area by throwing a line of track through some valley or across some river, often planning these moves a decade or more ahead. Little is known of the local economic and social results of this process beyond the fact that it extended railroad transportation at an extremely rapid rate.

Trying to assess the larger economic and social effects of Villard's activities, we might note that he mobilized about $60,000,000 in capital, and applied it to western development at a social cost of perhaps one or two million dollars. That is, he may have made more money than that, but the one or two million dollars represent an estimate of what he actually spent on living and personal durable goods during these years. His other money came and went in stockmarket operations, and presumably represented a transfer of capital from one set of holders to another. The question remains: granting that this was not a high rate of commission to pay for the mobilization of so much money, was the long-run effect of the development for which the money was spent economically and socially desirable? Undoubtedly, this particular development of transportation was premature, and it was carried on at the cost of some other types of goods or services that could have been produced with the same expenditure. But this in turn raises another question from a purely nationalistic standpoint: could the foreign capital have been attracted for more prosaic and routine operations? To the extent that foreign money was invested unprofitably in western development, it was an economic loss to Germany and the other investing nations, but a net gain to the United States. As to the loss of domestic resources in these developments, it can be noted that; at least, this is what the men of the culture apparently wanted to do with their economic energy. Villard noted in his promotion activities that the word "Oregon" had a kind of popular magic to it in the seventies and early eighties. Then it was the promised land of the American West, and it stimulated the imagination of Americans along entrepreneurial lines. The historian should try to assess the extent to which the dramatic development of natural resources may actually raise the rate of saving in the community, and may increase output of energy in the population as a whole. These are, of course, very difficult and intangible problems, but yet they are just as much a part of the picture of economic development as the old stand-by of assessing the value of natural resources and the cost of getting them to market.

There is a cultural paradox involved in all of this that makes it difficult for the unwary investigator. At the same time that Americans were saving at a high rate for development purposes and investing in railroad securities, they had a distrust of the railroad operator and were inclined to make the railroads a scapegoat for many of their ills. In other words, there was a kind of national Manicheaen heresy, whereby people were willing to sell themselves to the devil, to worship evil, as it were, but at the same time were not ready to forget the fact that it was really the devil and not good that they were supporting. This whole problem of ambiguity of attitude toward business leaders, and the reactions it led to on the part of the executives themselves, is one of the most fruitful fields of American cultural history.

IDA M. TARBELL (1857–1944), a journalist, served as an associate editor of *McClure's* and the *American* magazines during the Progressive period of the early twentieth century. Her most quoted work, *The History of the Standard Oil Company* (2 vols., 1904), first appeared in serial form in *McClure's* during the two years preceding 1904. While sounder in scholarship than earlier attacks on Rockefeller's empire, Tarbell's objectivity has been questioned, as her father and brother were executives of the Pure Oil combine of independent oil producers and refiners, competitors of the Standard Oil Company. In this selection, she criticizes the firm's competitive methods as unethical.*

John D.: The Ruthless Elimination of Competition

Mr. Rockefeller was certainly now in an excellent condition to work out his plan of bringing under his own control all the refineries of the country. The Standard Oil Company owned in each of the great refining centers, New York, Pittsburg and Philadelphia, a large and aggressive plant run by the men who had built it up. These works were, so far as the public knew, still independent and their only relation that of the "Central Association." As a matter of fact they were the "Central Association." Not only had Mr. Rockefeller brought these powerful interests into his concern; he had secured for them a rebate of ten per cent on a rate which should always be as low as any one of the roads gave any of his competitors. He had done away with middlemen, that is, he was "paying nobody a profit." He

had undeniably a force wonderfully constructed for what he wanted to do and one made practically impregnable as things were in the oil business then, by virtue of its special transportation rate.

As soon as his new line was complete the work of acquiring all outside refineries began at each of the oil centres. Unquestionably the acquisitions were made through persuasion when this was possible. If the party approached refused to lease or sell, he was told firmly what Mr. Rockefeller had told the Cleveland refiners when he went to them in 1872 with the South Improvement contracts, that there was no hope for him; that a combination was in progress which was bound to work; and that those who stayed out would inevitably go the wall. Naturally the first fruits to fall into the hands

*From Ida M. Tarbell, *The History of the Standard Oil Company* (New York: McClure-Phillips and Company, 1904), vol. I, pp. 154–166. Footnotes omitted.

of the new alliance were those refineries which were embarrassed or discouraged by the conditions which Mr. Rogers explains above. Take as an example the case of the Citizens' Oil Refining Company of Pittsburg, as it was explained in 1888 to the House Committee on Manufactures in its trust investigation. A. H. Tack, a partner in the company, told the story:

We began in 1869 with a capacity of 1,000 barrels a day. At the start everything was *couleur de rose,* so much so that we put our works in splendid shape. We manufactured all the products. We even got it down to making wax, and using the very last residuum in the boilers. We got the works in magnificent order and used up everything. We began to feel the squeeze in 1872. We did not know what was the matter. Of course we were all affected the same way in Pennsylvania, and of course we commenced shifting about, and meeting together, and forming delegations, and going down to Philadelphia to see the Pennsylvania Railroad, meeting after meeting and delegation after delegation. We suspected there was something wrong, and told those men there was something wrong somewhere; that we felt, so far as position was concerned, we had the cheapest barrels, the cheapest labour, and the cheapest coal, and the route from the crude district was altogether in our favour. We had a railroad and a river to bring us our raw material. We had made our investment based on the seaboard routes, and we wanted the Pennsylvania Railroad to protect us. But none of our meetings or delegations ever amounted to anything. They were always repulsed in some way, put off, and we never got any satisfaction. The consequence was that in two or three years there was no margin or profit. In order to overcome that we commenced speculating, in the hope that there would be a change some time or other for the better. We did not like the idea of giving up the ship. Now, during these times the Standard Oil Company increased so perceptibly and so strong that we at once recognised it as the element. Instead of looking to the railroad I always looked to the Standard Oil Company. In 1874 I went to see Rockefeller to find if we

could make arrangements with him by which we could run a portion of our works. It was a very brief interview. He said there was no hope for us at all. He remarked this—I cannot give the exact quotation—"There is no hope for us," and probably he said, "There is no hope for any of us", but he says, "The weakest must go first." And we went.

All over the country the refineries in the same condition as Mr. Tack's firm sold or leased. Those who felt the hard times and had any hope of weathering them resisted at first. With many of them the resistance was due simply to their love for their business and their unwillingness to share its control with outsiders. The thing which a man has begun, cared for, led to a healthy life, from which he has begun to gather fruit, which he knows he can make greater and richer, he loves as he does his life. It is one of the fruits of his life. He is jealous of it—wishes the honour of it, will not divide it with another. He can suffer heavily his own mistakes, learn from them, correct them. He can fight opposition, bear all—so long as the work is his. There were refiners in 1875 who loved their business in this way. Why one should love an oil refinery the outsider may not see; but to the man who had begun with one still and had seen it grow by his own energy and intelligence to ten, who now sold 500 barrels a day where he once sold five, the refinery was the dearest spot on earth save his home. He walked with pride among its evil-smelling places, watched the processes with eagerness, experimented with joy and recounted triumphantly every improvement. To ask such a man to give up his refinery was to ask him to give up the thing which, after his family, meant most in life to him.

To Mr. Rockefeller this feeling was a weak sentiment. To place love of independent work above love of profits was as incomprehensible to him as a refusal to accept a rebate because it was *wrong!* Where persuasion failed then, it was necessary, in his judgment, that pressure be applied—simply a pressure sufficient to demonstrate to these blind or recalcitrant individuals the impossibility of their long being able to do business independently. It was a pressure varied according to locality. Usually it took the form of cutting their market. The system of "predatory competition" was no invention of the Standard Oil Company. It prevailed in the oil business from the start. Indeed, it was one of the evils Mr. Rockefeller claimed his combination would cure, but until now it had been used spasmodically. Mr. Rockefeller never did anything spasmodically. He applied underselling for destroying his rivals' market with the same deliberation and persistency that characterised all his efforts, and in the long run he always won. There were other forms of pressure. Sometimes the independents found it impossible to get oil; again, they were obliged to wait days for cars to ship in; there seemed to be no end to the ways of making it hard for men to do business, of discouraging them until they would sell or lease, and always at the psychological moment a purchaser was at their side. Take as an example the case of the Harkness refinery in Philadelphia, a story told to the same committee as that of Mr. Tack:

"I was the originator of the enterprise," said William W. Harkness, "believing that there was no better place than Philadelphia to refine oil, particularly for export. We commenced then, as near as I can now recollect, about 1870, and we made money up to probably 1874. We managed our business very close and did not speculate in oil. We bought and we sold, and we paid a great deal of attention to the statistical part of our business so as to save waste, and we did a nice business.

But we found in some years that probably five months out of a year we could not sell our oil unless it would be at a positive loss, and then we stopped. Then when we could sell our oil, we found a difficulty about getting cars. My brother would complain of it, but I believed that the time would come when that would be equalised. I had no idea of the iniquity that was going on; I could not conceive it. I went on in good faith until about 1874, and then the trouble commenced. We could not get our oil and were compelled to sell at a loss. Then Warden, Frew and Company formed some kind of running arrangement where they supplied the crude, and we seemed to get along a little better. After a while the business got complicated, and I got tired and handed it over to my brother; I backed out. That was about 1875. I was dissatisfied and wanted to do an independent business, or else I wanted to give it up. In 1876—I recollect that very well, because it was the year of the Centennial Exposition—we were at the Centennial Exposition. I was sitting in front of the great Corliss engine, admiring it, and he told me there was a good opportunity to get out. Warden, Frew and Company, he said, were prepared to buy us out, and I asked him whether he considered that as the best thing to do; whether we had not better hold on and fight it through, for I believe that these difficulties would not continue; that we would get our oil. I knew he was a competent refiner, and I wanted to continue business, but he said he thought he had better make this arrangement, and I consented, and we sold out; we got our investment back."

Here we have a refiner discouraged by the conditions which Mr. Rockefeller claims his aggregation will cure. Under the Rutter circular and the discrimination in freight to the Standard which followed, his difficulty in getting oil increases, and he consents to a running arrangement with Mr. Rockefeller's partner in Philadelphia, but he wants to do an "independent business." Impossible. As he sits watching the smooth and terrible power of that famous Corliss engine of 1876, an engine which showed to thousands for the first time what great power properly directed means, he realised that something very like it was at work in the oil business—something resistless, silent, perfect in its might—and he sold out to that something. Everywhere men did the same. The history of oil refining on Oil Creek from 1875 to 1879 is almost uncanny. There were at the beginning of that period twenty-seven plants in the region, most of which were in a fair condition, considering the difficulties in the business. During 1873 the demand for refined oil had greatly increased, the exports nearly doubling over those of 1872. The average profit on refined that year in a well-managed refinery was not less than three cents a gallon. During the first half of 1874 the oil business had been depressed, but the oil refiners were looking for better times when the Rutter circular completely demoralised them by putting fifty cents extra freight charges on their shipments without an equivalent raise on competitive points. It was not only this extra charge, enough to cut off their profits, as business then stood, but it was that the same set of men who had thrown their business into confusion in 1872 was again at work. The announcement of the Central Association with Mr. Rockefeller's name at its head confirmed their fears. Nevertheless at first none of the small refiners would listen to the proposition to sell or lease made them in the spring of 1875 by the representative first sent out by the Central Association. They would have nothing to do, they said bluntly, with any combination engineered by John D. Rockefeller. The representative withdrew and the case was considered. In the mean time conditions on the creek grew harder. All sorts of difficulties began to be strewn in their way—

cars were hard to get, the markets they had built up were cut under them—a demoralising conviction was abroad in the trade that this new and mysterious combination was going to succeed; that it was doing rapidly what its members were reported to be saying daily: "We mean to secure the entire refining business of the world." Such was the state of things on the creek when in the early fall of 1875 an energetic young refiner and oil buyer well known in the Oil Regions, J. D. Archbold, appeared in Titusville as the representative of a new company, the Acme Oil Company, a concern which everybody believed to be an offshoot of the Standard Oil Company of Cleveland, though nobody could prove it. As a matter of fact the Acme was capitalised and controlled entirely by Standard men, its stockholders being, in addition to Mr. Archbold, William Rockefeller, William G. Warden, Frank Q. Barstow, and Charles Pratt. It was evident at once that the Acme Oil Company had come into the Oil Regions for the purpose of absorbing the independent interests as Mr. Rockefeller and his colleagues were absorbing them elsewhere. The work was done with a promptness and despatch which do great credit to the energy and resourcefulness of the engineer of the enterprise. In three years, by 1878, all but two of the refineries of Titusville had "retired from the business gloriously," as Mr. Archbold, flushed with victory, told the counsel of the Commonwealth of Pennsylvania in 1879, when the state authorities were trying to find what was at work in the oil interests to cause such a general collapse. Most of the concerns were bought outright, the owners being convinced that it was impossible for them to do an independent business, and being unwilling to try combination. All down the creek the little refineries which for years had faced every difficulty with stout hearts collapsed. "Sold out," "dismantled," "shut down," is the melancholy record of the industry during these four years. At the end practically nothing was left in the Oil Regions but the Acme of Titusville and the Imperial of Oil City, both of them now under Standard management. To the oil men this sudden wiping out of the score of plants with which they had been familiar for years seemed a crime which nothing could justify. Their bitterness of heart was only intensified by the sight of the idle refiners thrown out of business by the sale of their factories. These men had, many of them, handsome sums to invest, but what were they to put them in? They were refiners, and they carried a pledge in their pockets not to go into that business for a period of ten years. Some of them tried the discouraged oil man's fatal resource, the market, and as a rule left their money there. One refiner who had, according to popular report, received $200,000 for his business, speculated the entire sum away in less than a year. Others tried new enterprises, but men of forty learn new trades with difficulty, and failure followed many of them. The scars left in the Oil Regions by the Standard Combination of 1875–1879 are too deep and ugly for men and women of this generation to forget them.

In Pittsburg the same thing was happening. At the beginning of the work of absorption—1874—there were between twenty-two and thirty refineries in the town. As we have seen, Lockhart and Frew sold to the Standard Oil Company of Cleveland some time in 1874. In the fall of that year a new company was formed in Pittsburg, called the Standard Oil Company of Pittsburg. Its president was Charles Lockhard; its directors William Frew, David Bushnell, H. M. Flagler, and W. G. Warden—all members of the Standard Oil Company and four of them stockholders in the South Improvement Company. This company at once began to lease or buy refineries. Many of the Pittsburg refiners made a valiant fight to get rates on their oil which would enable them to run independently. To save expense they tried to bring oil from the oil fields by barge; the pipe-lines in the pool refused to run oil to barges, the railroad to accept oil brought down by barge. An independent pipe-line attempted to bring it to Pittsburg, but to reach the works the pipe-line must run under a branch of the Pennsylvania railroad. It refused to permit this, and for months the oil from the line was hauled in wagons from the point where it had been held up, over the railroad track, and there repiped and carried to Pittsburg. At every point they met interference until finally one by one they gave in. According to Mr. Frew, who in 1879 was examined as to the condition of things in Pittsburg, the company began to "acquire refiners" in 1875. In 1877 they bought their last one; and at the time Mr. Frew was under examination he could not remember but *one* refinery in operation in Pittsburg not controlled by his company.

Nor was it refiners only who sold out. All departments of the trade began to yield to the pressure. There was in the oil business a class of men known as shippers. They bought crude oil, sent it East, and sold it to refineries there. Among the largest of these was Adnah Neyhart, whose active representative was W. T. Scheide. Now to Mr. Rockefeller the independent shipper was an incubus; he did a business which, in his judgment, a firm ought to do for itself, and reaped a profit which might go direct into the business. Besides, so long as there were shippers to supply crude to the Eastern refineries at living prices, so long these concerns might resist offers to sell or lease.

Some time in the fall of 1872 Mr. Scheide began to lose his customers in New York. He found that they were making some kind of working arrangement with the Standard Oil Company, just what he did not know. But at all events they no longer bought from him but from the Standard buyer, J. A. Bostwick and Company. At the same time he became convinced that Mr. Rockefeller was after his business. "I knew that they were making some strenuous efforts to get our business," he told the Hepburn Commission in 1879, "because I used to meet Mr. Rockefeller in the Erie office." At the same time that he was facing the loss of customers and the demoralising conviction that the Standard Oil Company wanted his business, he was experiencing more or less disgust over business conditions in New York. "I did not like the character of my customers there," Mr. Scheide told the committee. "I did not think they were treating us fairly and squarely. There was a strong competition in handling oil. The competition had got to be so strong that 'outside refiners,' as they called themselves then, used to go around bidding up the price of their works on the Standard Oil Company, and they were using me to sell their refineries to the Standard. They would say to refiners: 'Neyhard will do so and so, and we are going to continue running.' And they would say to us that the Standard was offering lower prices. I recollect one instance in which they, after having made a contract to buy oil from me if I would bring it over the Erie Railway, broke that contract for the 1-128th part of a cent a gallon. I sold out the next week." When Mr. Scheide went to the freight agent of

the Erie road, Mr. Blanchard, and told him of his decision to sell, Mr. Blanchard tried to dissuade him. During the conversation he let out a fact that must have convinced Mr. Scheide more fully than ever that he had been wise in determining to give up his business. Mr. Blanchard told him as a reason for his staying and trusting to the Erie road to keep its contacts with him that the Standard Oil Company had been offering him five cents more a barrel than Mr. Scheide was paying them, and would take all their cars, and load them all regularly if they would throw him over and give them the business. It is interesting to note that when Mr. Scheide sold in the spring of 1875, it was, as he supposed, to Charles Pratt and Company. Well informed as he was in all the intricacies of the business—and there were few abler or more energetic men in trade at the time—he did not know that Charles Pratt and Company had been part and parcel of the Standard Oil Company since October, 1874.

Of course securing a large crude shipping business like Mr. Neyhart's was a valuable point for the Standard. It threw all of the refiners whom he had supplied out of crude oil and forced several of them to come to the Standard buyer—a first step, of course, toward a lease or sale. At every point, indeed, making it difficult for the refiner to get his raw product was one of the favourite manoeuvres of the combination. It was not only to crude oil it was applied. Factories which worked up the residuum or tar into lubricating oil and depended on Standard plants for their supply were cut off. There was one such in Cleveland—the firm of Morehouse and Freeman. Mr. Morehouse had begun to experiment with lubricating oils in 1861, and in 1871 the report of the Cleveland Board of Trade devoted several of its pages to a description of his business. According to this account he was then making oils adapted to lubricating all kinds of machinery—he held patents for several brands and trade marks, and had produced that year over 25,000 barrels of different lubricants besides 120,000 boxes of axle grease. At this time he was buying his stock or residuum from one or another of the twenty-five Cleveland refiners. Then came the South Improvement Company and the concentration of the town's refining interest in Mr. Rockefeller's hands. Mr. Morehouse, according to the testimony he gave the Hepburn Commission in 1879, went to Mr. Rockefeller, after the consolidation, to arrange for supplies. He was welcomed—the Standard Oil Company had not at that time begun to deal in lubricating oils—and encouraged to build a new plant. This was done at a cost of $41,000, and a contract was made with the Standard Oil Company for a daily supply of eighty-five barrels of residuum. Some time in 1874 this supply was cut down to twelve barrels. The price was put up too, and contracts for several months were demanded so that Mr. Morehouse got no advantage from the variation in crude prices. Then the freights went up on the railroads. He paid $1.50 and two dollars for what he says he felt sure his big neighbour was paying but seventy or seventy-five cents (there is no evidence of any such low rate to the Standard from Cleveland to New York by rail). Now it was impossible for Mr. Morehouse to supply his trade on twelve barrels of stock. He begged Mr. Rockefeller for more. It was there in the Standard Oil works. Why could he not have it? He could pay for it. He and his partner offered to buy 5,000 barrels and store it, but Mr. Rockefeller was firm. All he could give Mr. Morehouse was twelve barrels a day. "I saw readily what that meant," said Mr. Morehouse, "that meant squeeze you out—buy your works. They have got the works and are running them; I am without anything. They paid about $15,000 for what cost me $41,000. He said that he had facilities for freighting and that the coal-oil business belonged to them; and any concern that would start in that business, they had sufficient money to lay aside a fund to wipe them out—these are the words."

At every refining centre in the country this process of consolidation through persuasion, intimidation, or force, went on. As fast as a refinery was brought in line its work was assigned to it. If it was an old and poorly equipped plant it was usually dismantled or shut down. If it was badly placed, that is, if it was not economically placed in regard to a pipe-line and railroad, it was dismantled even though in excellent condition. If it was a large and well-equipped plant advantageously located it was assigned a certain quota to manufacture, and it did nothing but manufacture. The buying of crude, the making of freight rates, the selling of the output remained with Mr. Rockefeller. The contracts under which all the refineries brought into line were run were of the most detailed and rigid description, and they were executed as a rule with a secrecy which baffles description. Take, for example, a running arrangement made by Rockefeller in 1876, with a Cleveland refinery, that of Scofield, Shurmer and Teagle. The members of this concern had all been in the refining business in Cleveland in 1872 and had all handed over their works to Mr. Rockefeller, when he notified them of the South Improvement Company's contracts. Mr. Shurmer declared once in an affidavit that he alone lost $20,000 by that manoeuvre. The members of the firm had not stayed out of business, however. Recovering from the panic caused by the South Improvement Company, they had united in 1875, building a refinery worth $65,000, with a yearly capacity of 180,000 barrels of crude. On the first year's business they made $40,000. Although this was doing well, they were convinced they might do better if they could get as good freight rates as the Standard Oil Company, and in the spring of 1876 they brought suit against the Lake Shore and Michigan Southern and the New York Central and Hudson River Railroads for "unlawful and unjust discrimination, partialities and preferences made and practised . . . in favour of the Standard Oil Company, enabling the said Standard Oil Company to obtain to a great extent the monopoly of the oil and naphtha trade of Cleveland." The suit was not carried through at the time, Mr. Rockefeller seems to have suggested a surer way to the firm of getting the rates they wanted. This was to make a running arrangement with him. He seems to have demonstrated to them that they could make more money under his plan than outside, and they signed a contract for a remarkable "joint adventure." According to this document Scofield, Shurmer and Teagle put into the business a plant worth at that time about $73,000 and their entire time. Mr. Rockefeller put in $10,000 and his rebates! That is, he secured for the firm the same preferential rates on their shipments that the Standard Oil Company enjoyed. The firm bound itself not to refine over 85,000 barrels a year and neither jointly nor separately to engage in any other form of oil business for ten years— the life of the contract. Scofield, Shurmer and Teagle were guaranteed a profit of $35,000 a year. Profits over $35,000 went to Mr. Rockefeller up to $70,000; any further profits were divided.

The making of this contract and its execution were attended by all the secret rites peculiar to Mr. Rockefeller's business ventures. According to the testimony of one of the firm given a few years later on the witness stand in Cleveland the contract was signed at night at Mr. Rockefeller's house on Euclid Avenue in Cleveland, where he told the gentlemen that they must not tell even their wives about the new arrangement, that if they made money they must conceal it—they were not to drive fast horses, "put on style," or do anything to let people suspect there were unusual profits in oil refining. That would invite competition. They were told that all accounts were to be kept secret. Fictitious names were to be used in corresponding, and a special box at the post-office was employed for these fictitious characters. In fact, smugglers and housebreakers never surrounded their operations with more mystery.

But make his operations as thickly as he might in secrecy, the effect of Mr. Rockefeller's steady and united attack on the refining business was daily becoming more apparent. Before the end of 1876 the alarm among oil producers, the few independent refineries still in business, and even in certain railroad circles was serious. On all sides talk of a united effort to meet the consolidation was heard.

RALPH W. HIDY (b. 1905) since 1957 has been Isidor
Straus Professor of Business History at the Harvard
Graduate School of Business Administration. Besides
the history of Standard Oil from which this selection
is taken, he has written *The House of Bàring in
American Trade and Finance* (1949), coauthored
Timber and Men, The Weyerhauser Story (1963),
and is working on a history of the Great Northern
Railroad. MURIEL HIDY is his wife and frequent
collaborator. The Hidys represent what economic
historians call the Harvard Group, a body of scholars
who during the last forty years have directed their
energies to the study of decision making within business
firms. They measure the role of the businessman by
economic results instead of social values, and in this
selection hold that while the Standard Oil management
used unrelenting pressure on competitors, their
dominant position came from efficiency rather than
ruthlessness. Is efficiency more important than ethics
in business decisions?*

Ralph W. and Muriel Hidy

Consolidation Through Efficiency

Policies and practices pursued by Standard Oil executives during the years prior to 1882 emerged in a variety of ways. Some policies were evidenced by votes of directors of components of the alliance and gradually won more general acceptance among its members. In other instances precedents and practices developed into policies over time; no formalized statement ever indicated the direction in which the leaders were traveling, but in a succession of separate steps they evolved a significant behavior pattern.

Many of the concepts and procedures adopted by executives of the alliance stemmed from their early experience as small businessmen. Probably at no other time during the nineteenth century was economic activity more freely competitive than in the period from 1840 to 1865. The customs and mores of the small individual enterpriser became the accepted pattern for almost all men. Naturally enough, therefore, Rockefeller and his associates learned in their youth to believe in freedom of entry into any occupation, in the sanctity of private property, in the obligation of the owner to manage his own operations, and in the right to keep his business affairs secret, a concept dating from time immemorial. As a corollary of that idea, in courts or legislative investigative chambers a businessman testified to the legal truth, and no more, a practice still honored by general observance in spite of critical charges of evasiveness and ambiguity. Since most markets were local, every businessman could observe his competitors with relative ease, and did. His habit was to use any competitive device not clearly prohibited by law. Bargaining in the market place was almost universal, whether for products or for such services as the transportation of freight. Posted prices were a point of departure for haggling, and price reductions were the most widely utilized of competitive techniques.

In response to the chaotic and depressed years of the 1870's, however, Standard Oil men drastically modified some of their socially inherited concepts about competition. They apparently desired at first to bring all gatherers of crude oil and refiners of light petroleum fractions into one commonly owned unit—to create a monopoly. Late in the decade they added lubricating oil specialists and trunk pipelines to their list of components to be unified. By means of common ownership in an association of specializing firms, Rockefeller and his associates created a great horizontal and vertical combination, which, on the eve of the birth of Jersey Standard, maintained overwhelming dominance in gathering, storing, and processing petroleum and its derivatives.

Either by design or through pressure of circumstances, the Standard Oil group of executives had not achieved monopoly in any function by 1881. Strong minority interests in many domestic marketing companies within the alliance, and limited coverage of the market by them, set definite limits to the influence of top managers in that field of operations. In almost all sales for export foreign merchants bought oil from companies in the Standard Oil family and carried on marketing in foreign lands. The combination owned few producing properties. United Pipe Lines men failed to keep pace with expansion in Bradford production, and competing gathering and storing facilities kept appearing. Tide-Water Pipe had thrown the first trunk pipeline over the mountains toward the sea and remained a belligerent competitor. Under the agreement with the producers in 1880 the price of crude oil was set on the oil exchanges, not by Standard Oil. In manufacturing, the area of initial intent for monopoly, the top managers of the alliance had stopped short of their goal. They had refused to pay the prices asked by owners of some plants. Others had sprung up in response to inducements offered by the Pennsylvania Railroad, and in 1882 the editor of *Mineral Resources* noted that the combination had "for some reason" not renewed leases on a number of refineries, several of which were doing "a good trade" and "assuming considerable importance." Thus, by that year some of the firms classified by H. H. Rogers in 1879 as being "in harmony" with Standard Oil had gone their independent ways.

Standard Oil executives employed a variety of tactics in carrying out the expansionist program during the 1870's. After the consolidation in Cleveland and the disastrous South Improvement episode, Rockefeller and his associates first won the confidence of competitors through comprehensive voluntary association. They then brought into the alliance the strongest men and firms in specific areas or functions, a policy pursued, with some exceptions, until 1911. Exchange of stock in the different companies by individuals and guarantee of equality in management provided the final assurance needed to convince such strong individualists as Lockhart, Warden, Pratt, and Rogers that combination was to their advantage. All then co-operated eagerly in trying to unify the remaining firms in refining by bringing them into The Central Association, by buying plants whenever feasible, and by leasing other works. If a seller personally chose not to enter the combination, he usually signed an agreement not to engage in the petroleum business for a period of years. In any case, evidence in extant records substantiates the point that Standard Oil men completely and carefully inventoried all properties and paid "good," though not high, prices for them, including compensation for patents, trademarks, brands, good-will, and volume of business. In many instances prices for properties reflected the desire of Standard Oil officials to enlist the inventive capacities or administrative abilities of the owners in the service of the alliance. The preponderance of the evidence indicates that Rockefeller and his fellow executives preferred to buy out rather than fight out competitors.

At the same time, when Standard Oil men felt it necessary to apply pressure as a means of persuading a rival to lease or sell his plant, they showed no hesitancy in utilizing the usual sharp competitive practices prevailing in the oil industry during the 1870's. On one occasion or another they pre-empted all available staves and barrels, restricted as completely as possible the available tank cars to their own business, and indulged in local price cutting. They meticulously watched and checked on competitive shipments and sales, sometimes in co-operation with railroad men, and diligently negotiated advantageous freight rates on railways, even to the point of receiving rebates or drawbacks on rivals' shipments. All acts were kept secret as long as possible. The size and resources of the alliance gave it overwhelming power, which was sometimes used ruthlessly, though it is worthy of note that numerous oilmen successfully resisted the pressure.

Within the alliance itself executives also retained many of their competitive habits. Although price competition almost completely disappeared within the combination, men and firms raced with each other in reducing costs, devising new techniques, developing products, improving their quality, and showing profits. Top managers believed in competition but not in the undisciplined variety.

In building the alliance the leaders of Standard Oil adopted a long-range view with emphasis on planning, even before they had achieved an organization to carry such an approach into successful operation. They showed a profound faith in the permanence of the industry, a belief not generally held in years when the petroleum business was characterized by instability, rapid exhaustion of producing fields, and doubts about the appearance of new ones. They wanted to plan and to have reasonable assurance that they were taking no more than calculated risks in pushing toward their objectives. A necessary requirement of planning was centralized policy formulation.

That responsibility devolved not upon one man but on a group of executives. The evolution of Standard Oil's committee system, the hallmark of its administrative methods, started early in the seventies. The original bylaws of Ohio Standard provided for an Executive Committee. Its first membership of two, John D. Rockefeller and Flagler, was increased to three during the consecutive terms of Samuel Andrews and O. H. Payne. Archbold replaced the latter in 1879. William Rockefeller, Pratt, Warden, and Bostwick had joined the three Cleveland members the previous year. At that time the Executive Committee absorbed the "Advisory Committee," which had been established as early as 1873 to act in the New York area. William Rockefeller and Bostwick, its first members, had been joined by Pratt and Warden soon after they entered the alliance. The enlarged Executive Committee of 1878 held many of its almost daily meetings at 140 Pearl Street, New York, and two years later made four a quorum because of the geographic split in membership between Cleveland and New York. Members of other committees, to be discussed in the next chapter, started consultations before 1882. If the making of decisions as a synthesis of opinion of a group after discussion is a characteristic of modern business, as a recent commentator has implied, then Standard Oil was modern in the 1870's.

In order to have easily available the best data and advice for making decisions, the Rockefellers and their associates built up staffs in Cleveland, New York, and other points. For the use of executives they collected, evaluated, and digested information on crude oil supplies, costs of manufacture, and markets all over the world. The practice of watching and reporting on marketing by competitors everywhere in the United States, not merely locally, was already inaugurated, though not yet systematized. S. C. T. Dodd was engaged as legal navigator; Standard Oil officials desired to operate within the law. A beginning was made in standardizing accounting procedures.

As the emergence of the Executive Committee and the formation of staffs indicated, the creation of the combination permitted a division of labor or specialization within the organization. As Archbold expressed the development in 1888, the grouping of talents within the alliance permitted "various individuals to take up the different features of the business as a specialty and accomplish greater efficiency than can possibly be accomplished by an individual who attempts to cover all in a business."

In the matter of finance, as in other aspects of operations, Ohio Standard set precedents on reporting and central review. In 1877 the directors of that company resolved that all persons responsible for different aspects of the business should make quarterly reports in writing to the board. Two years later, its members unanimously agreed that annual financial statements should be presented. In 1875 the directors had voted that expenditures for new construction in manufacturing exceeding $2,500 should be undertaken only with written consent of seven members of the board, but that resolution was repealed five years later and the company's Executive Committee was given full charge of all matters relating to repairs and new construction.

Since the goal of the members of the alliance was to maximize profits in the long run, they adopted practices to that end. Emphasis was placed on reducing costs, improving and standardizing the quality of products, and striving for new methods of refining, including the engaging of specialists. Stories about John D. Rockefeller's penchant for eliminating waste and effecting economies have been told and retold. As president of the Acme Oil Company in the Oil Regions, Archbold achieved substantial savings through buying supplies in quantity and by making annual contracts regarding the repairing of boilers and barrels for all plants under his jurisdiction. When he purchased a lubricating oil patent in 1879, Archbold guaranteed the owner, Eli E. Hendrick, a salary of $10,000 per year for ten years in return for the devotion of his inventive talents to Acme. Duplicating pipelines were removed, inefficient plants dismantled, strategically located refineries enlarged, and auxiliary manufacturing units developed, all in the name of economy and reduction of costs. By consistently stressing that practice in every function

Standard Oil men moved gradually but inevitably toward mass manufacturing and, more slowly, toward mass marketing.

Gathering information, consultation, planning, and experimentation did not always lead to quick action, but the leaders of Standard Oil early indicated flexibility in adopting new methods and thoroughness in carrying them out. Critics voiced the opinion in the late 1870's that Standard Oil, having invested so much in refineries in the Oil Regions, could not take advantage of the pipeline revolution to establish large manufacturing units at the coast. Almost as soon as others had demonstrated the feasibility of building long trunk pipelines the Standard Oil group took action in 1879. It already possessed a system of gathering lines through the United Pipe Lines. After its organization in 1881, the National Transit Company pushed trunk pipeline building vigorously. By the next year it owned 1,062 miles of trunk lines, only 48 of which had been bought from firms outside the alliance. Its policies, enlarged upon in later chapters, illustrate the fact that Standard Oil was not always the earliest to initiate an innovation, but, once launched on a policy, the combination pushed it with vigor and fervor made possible by efficient organization and ample financial resources.

Standard Oil's financial policy itself was an important element in the successful life of the combination and its components. Not only were the risks spread by the breadth of the alliance's activities, but profits made in one company or phase of the business flowed into development of another when desired. Early in the history of Standard Oil units short-term loans were often obtained from commercial banks, and temporary aid had to be obtained when the properties of The Empire Transportation Company were purchased. A conservative ratio of dividends to net income, however, was soon to permit the accumulation of funds for self-financing.

Ohio Standard furnished an example for the companies in the alliance on the matter of insurance against fire. On the assumption that loss by fire was a normal expense of the petroleum industry and could be carried by a large unit, the directors of the Ohio Company agreed in January, 1877, to insure property in any one place only on the excess of its valuation above $100,000.

As directors of The Standard Oil Company (Ohio), executives of the alliance also set a precedent regarding the ownership of producing properties. In April, 1878, apparently as a result of a suit by H. L. Taylor & Company against John D. Rockefeller and others for breach of contract in a joint producing operation, the directors unanimously voted not to invest any more money in the purchase of crude oil lands. Six months later they resolved to discontinue all activity in producing petroleum and instructed the Executive Committee to dispose of its properties. This point of view had an influence upon the Standard Oil alliance for a decade.

Quite the contrary was the action adopted in regard to pipelines. By 1881 the Standard Oil group was definitely launched on a program for large-scale expansion of its pipeline facilities and soon exercised a greater measure of control over the function. The combination poured an increasing quantity of capital into building lines; the profits from them provided a cushion for all operations of the alliance. The speculatively minded can ask whether the development of the oil industry would have been more rapid or socially beneficial had parallel pipelines competed with each other during the formative years of the industry, and whether the development would have been as efficient, or more so, had the railroad systems controlled competing lines, as had seemed possible in the 1870's. The point remains that the top managers of Standard Oil determined to keep this function in their own hands to the extent possible; the measure of success achieved is discussed later.

The roots of Standard Oil's policies went deep into the personalities and early experiences of Rockefeller and his associates. Though few of their practices had been satisfactorily systematized by 1881, precedents had been established for many later policies of Jersey Standard and other members of the combination.

By the end of 1881 the general public was hard put to make an accurate estimate of Standard Oil's behavior. Legislative investigations and several legal cases had already elicited an enormous amount of conflicting testimony as to the relations of the combination with both railroads and competitors. Rockefeller and his associates had heightened un-certainty and speculation about their activities by their secrecy in building the alliance and by their evasive, often ambiguous, consistently legally accurate testimony on the witness stand. The very newness, size, dominance, and efficiency of the combination, not to mention its absorption of small competitors in adversity and its avid search for the lowest possible railroad rates, all tended to arouse antagonism. In 1882 S. H. Stowell closed his comments on Standard Oil in *Mineral Resources* with an unbiased observer's puzzlement: "There seems to be little doubt that the company has done a great work, and that through its instrumentality oil refining has been reduced to a business, and transportation has been greatly simplified; but as to how much evil has been mixed with this good, it is not practicable to make a definite statement." It was certain that through combination managers of Standard Oil had brought a measure of order to a formerly confused industry, though they thought that the administration of the alliance itself needed further systematization.

RICHARD HOFSTADTER (b. 1916), DeWitt Clinton Professor of American History at Columbia University, ranks as one of the outstanding historians in the United States. This selection comes from his first book, *Social Darwinism in American Thought* (1944), a work he followed with more than ten others, including two Pulitzer Prize winners, *The Age of Reform* (1955) and *Anti-intellectualism in American Life* (1963). Hofstadter views Social Darwinism as dominating the climate of opinion during the Gilded Age, with the philosophy of Herbert Spencer affecting all who came in contact with it, including the captains of industry.*

Richard Hofstadter

The Pervasive Influence of Social Darwinism

"The peculiar condition of American society," wrote Henry Ward Beecher to Herbert Spencer in 1866, "has made your writings far more fruitful and quickening here than in Europe." Why Americans were disposed to open their minds to Spencer, Beecher did not say; but there is much to substantiate his words. Spencer's philosophy was admirably suited to the American scene. It was scientific in derivation and comprehensive in scope. It had a reassuring theory of progress based upon biology and physics. It was large enough to be all things to all men, broad enough to satisfy agnostics like Robert Ingersoll and theists like Fiske and Beecher. It offered a comprehensive world-view, uniting under one generaliza-tion everything in nature from protozoa to politics. Satisfying the desire of "advanced thinkers" for a world-system to replace the shattered Mosaic cosmogony, it soon gave Spencer a public influence that transcended Darwin's. Moreover it was not a technical creed for professionals. Presented in language that tyros in philosophy could understand, it made Spencer the metaphysician of the homemade intellectual, and the prophet of the cracker-barrel agnostic. Although its influence far outstripped its merits, the Spencerian system serves students of the American mind as a fossil specimen from which the intellectual body of the period may be reconstructed. Oliver Wendell Holmes hardly exaggerated when he ex-

*From Richard Hofstadter, *Social Darwinism in American Thought*, pp. 31–35, 44–46, 48–49. Reprinted by permission of the Beacon Press, copyright © 1944, 1955 by the American Historical Association. Footnotes omitted.

pressed his doubt that "any writer of English except Darwin has done so much to affect our whole way of thinking about the universe."

When Spencer's philosophy was winning its way in America, transcendentalism was in its twilight and the newer philosophical idealism inspired by Hegel was barely apparent on the horizon. Pragmatism was just emerging in the minds of Chauncey Wright and the little-appreciated Charles Peirce. The latter's now-famous article, "How to Make Our Ideas Clear," appeared in 1878, fourteen years after the first volume of Spencer's *Synthetic Philosophy;* and James's epoch-making California Union address, the opening gun in the campaign to popularize pragmatism, did not come until 1898. In the history of the American mind, however, the *Synthetic Philosophy* (which appeared in a series of volumes after 1860) is more than a colorless tenant of the vacancy between transcendentalism and pragmatism; although Emerson called Spencer a "stock writer" and James hurled at the Victorian Aristotle some of his sharpest barbs, Spencer was to most of his educated American contemporaries a great man, a grand intellect, a giant figure in the history of thought.

The ground for an American reception of Spencer's philosophy was well prepared in New England, which was, if one may judge by prominent persons among those answering Youmans' solicitations for advance subscribers to the volumes of the *Synthetic Philosophy,* the nursery of Spencerian influence. The presence on early subscription lists of such names as George Bancroft, Edward Everett, John Fiske, Asa Gray, Edward Everett Hale, James Russell Lowell, Wendell Phillips, Jared Sparks, Charles Sumner, and George Ticknor attests the power of New England intellectualism to provide for Spencer an American audience. The effect of transcendentalism and Unitarianism in breaking up old orthodoxies and liberating the minds of American intellectuals cannot be measured but may certainly be sensed by any student of post-Civil War intellectual trends. Indeed, Americans were responsible for Spencer's chance to continue turning out the successive volumes of his project. In 1865, when the small returns from sales of his first volumes threatened to compel Spencer to give up his work, Youmans raised the necessary $7,000 among sympathetic Americans.

Within a few years of his announcement of the *Synthetic Philosophy,* Spencer's work was known to a considerable body of American readers. The *Atlantic Monthy* commented in 1864:

Mr. Herbert Spencer is already a power in the world. . . . He has already influenced the silent life of a few thinking men whose belief marks the point to which the civilization of the age must struggle to rise. In America, we may even now confess our obligations to the writings of Mr. Spencer, for here sooner than elsewhere the mass feel as utility what a few recognize as truth. . . . Mr. Spencer represents the scientific spirit of the age. He makes note of all that comes within the range of sensuous experience, and declares whatever may be derived therefrom by careful induction. As a philosopher he does not go farther. . . .Mr. Spencer has already established principles which, however compelled for a time to compromise with prejudices and vested interests, will become the recognized basis of an improved society.

In the three decades after the Civil War it was impossible to be active in any field of intellectual work without mastering Spencer. Almost every American philosophical thinker of first or second rank—notably James, Royce, Dewey, Bowne, Harris, Howison, and McCosh—had to reckon with Spencer at some time. He had a vital influence upon most of the founders of American sociology, especially Ward, Cooley, Giddings, Small, and Sumner. "I imagine that nearly all of us who took up sociology between 1870, say, and 1890 did so at the instigation of Spencer," acknowledged Cooley. He continued:

His book, *The Study of Sociology,* perhaps the most readable of all his works, had a large sale and probably did more to arouse interest in the subject than any other publication before or since. Whatever we may have occasion to charge against him, let us set down at once a large credit for effective propagation.

The Appleton publications, under the leadership of Youmans, pressed Spencer's interest incessantly, with the result that articles by him or about him were sprinkled throughout the popular magazines. The generation that acclaimed Grant as its hero took Spencer as its thinker. "Probably no other philosopher," wrote Henry Holt in later years,

. . . ever had such a vogue as Spencer had from about 1870 to 1890. Most preceding philosophers had presumably been mainly restricted to readers habitually given to the study of philosophy, but not only was Spencer considerably read and generally talked about by the whole intelligent world in England and America, but that world was wider than any that preceded it.

Spencer's impact upon the common man in the United States is impossible to gauge, although its effects are dimly perceptible. That he was widely read by persons who were partly or largely self-educated, by those who were laboriously plodding their way out of theological orthodoxy in a thousand towns and hamlets, is suggested by casual references to him in the lives of men who later achieved some fame. Theodore Dreiser, Jack London, Clarence Darrow, and Hamlin Garland have given intimations of Spencer's influence on their formative years. John R. Commons, in his autobiography, remarks on the fascination Spencer had for his father's friends during the writer's Indiana boyhood:

He and his cronies talked politics and science. Every one of them in that Eastern section of Indiana was a Republican, living on the battle cries of the Civil War, and every one was a follower of Herbert Spencer, who was then the shining light of evolution and individualism. Several years later, in 1888, I was shocked, at a meeting of the American Economic Association, to hear Professor Ely denounce Herbert Spencer who had misled economists. I was brought up on Hoosierism, Republicanism, Presbyterianism, and Spencerism.

The sales of Spencer's books in America from their earliest publication in the 1860's to December 1903 came to 368,755 volumes, a figure probably unparalleled for works in such difficult spheres as philosophy and sociology. The number of persons who fell under his influence must be measured also by the extent to which copies were passed from hand to hand, and circulated through libraries. Of course it is impossible to say that the acceptance of his ideas was proportionate to their circulation. Certainly there was no lack of criticism. A *Nation* reviewer commented in 1884, before the vogue was over, that "the books examining or refuting Spencer now make an imposing library." This criticism itself was another measure of the man's towering influence. . . .

With its rapid expansion, its exploitative methods, its desperate competition, and its peremptory rejection of failure, post-bellum America was like a vast human caricature of the Darwinian struggle for existence and survival of the fittest. Successful business entrepreneurs apparently accepted almost by instinct the Darwinian terminology which seemed to portray the conditions of their existence. Businessmen are not commonly articulate social philosophers, but a rough reconstruction of their social outlook shows how congenial to their thinking were the plausible analogies of social selection, and how welcome was the expansive evolutionary optimism of the Spencerian system. In a nation permeated with the gospel of progress, the incentive of pecuniary success appealed even to many persons whose ethical horizons were considerably broader than those of business enterprise. "I perceive clearly," wrote Walt Whitman in *Democratic Vistas,* "that the extreme business energy, and this almost maniacal appetite for wealth prevalent in the United States, are parts of amelioration and progress, indispensably needed to prepare the very results I demand. My theory includes riches, and the getting of riches . . ." No doubt there were many to applaud the assertion of the railroad executive Chauncey Depew that the guests at the great dinners and public banquets of New York City represented the survival of the fittest of the thousands who came there in search of fame, fortune, or power, and that it was "superior ability, foresight, and adaptability" that brought them successfully through the fierce competitions of the metropolis. James J. Hill, another railroad magnate, in an essay defending business consolidation, argued that "the fortunes of railroad companies are determined by the law of the survival of the fittest," and implied that the absorption of smaller by larger roads represents the industrial analogy to the victory of the strong. And John D. Rockefeller, speaking from an intimate acquaintance with the methods of competition, declared in a Sunday-school address:

> The growth of a large business is merely a survival of the fittest. . . . The American Beauty rose can be produced in the splendor and fragrance which bring cheer to its beholder only by sacrificing the early buds which grow up around it. This is not an evil tendency in business. It is merely the working-out of a law of nature and a law of God.

The most prominent of the disciples of Spencer was Andrew Carnegie, who sought out the philosopher, became his intimate friend, and showered him with favors. In his autobiography, Carnegie told how troubled and perplexed he had been over the collapse of Christian theology, until he took the trouble to read Darwin and Spencer.

> I remember that light came as in a flood and all was clear. Not only had I got rid of theology and the supernatural, but I had found the truth of evolution. "All is well since all grows better," became my motto, my true source of comfort. Man was not created with an instinct for his own degradation, but from the lower he had risen to the higher forms. Nor is there any conceivable end to his march to perfection. His face is turned to the light; he stands in the sun and looks upward.

Perhaps it was comforting, too, to discover that social laws were founded in the immutable principles of the natural order. In an article in the *North American Review,* which he ranked among the best of his writings, Carnegie emphasized the biological foundations of the law of competition. However much we may object to the seeming harshness of this law, he wrote, "It is here; we cannot evade it; no substitutes for it have been found; and while the law may sometimes be hard for the individual, it is best for the race, because it insures the survival of the fittest in every department." Even if it might be desirable for civilization eventually to discard its individualistic foundation, such a change is not practicable in our age; it would belong to another "long succeeding sociological stratum," whereas our duty is with the here and now.

The reception accorded to Spencer's social ideas cannot be dissociated from that accorded to the main body of his thought; however some part of his success probably came because he was telling the guardians of American society what they wanted to hear. Grangers, Greenbackers, Single Taxers, Knights of Labor, trade unionists, Populists, Socialists Utopian and Marxian—all presented challenges to the existing pattern of free enterprise, demanded reforms by state action, or insisted upon a thorough remodeling of the social order. Those who wished to continue in established ways were pressed for a theoretical answer to the rising voices of criticism. Said ironmaster Abram S. Hewitt:

> The problem presented to systems of religion and schemes of government is, to make men who are equal in liberty—that is, in political rights and therefore entitled to the ownership of property—content with that inequality in its distribution which must inevitably result from the application of the law of justice.

This problem the Spencerian system could solve. . . .

The peak of Spencer's American popularity probably was reached in the fall of 1882, when he made a memorable visit to the United States. In spite of his aversion to reporters, Spencer received much attention from the press, and hotel managers and railway agents competed for the privilege of serving him. Finally yielding one synthetic "interview" with the gentle-men of the press, Spencer expressed (it was a slightly jarring note) his fear that the American character was not sufficiently developed to make the best use of its republican institutions. The prospect for the future, however, was encouraging; from "biological truths," he told the reporters, he inferred that the eventual mixture of the allied varieties of the Aryan race forming the population would produce "a finer type of man than has hitherto existed." Whatever difficulties the Americans might have to surmount, they might "reasonably look forward to a time when they will have produced a civilization grander than any the world has known."

The climax of the visit was a hastily arranged banquet at Delmonico's, which gave American notables an opportunity to pay personal tribute. The dinner was attended by leaders in American letters, science, politics, theology, and business. Spencer's message to this distinguished audience was somewhat disappointing. He had observed, he said, an excess of hurry and hard labor in the tempo of American life, too much of the gospel of work; his friends would ruin their constitutions with exertion. The guests rewarded this appeal against strenuosity with a strenuous round of fulsome tributes, which painfully embarrassed even the vain Spencer. William Graham Sumner ascribed the foundations of sociological method to the guest of honor; Carl Schurz suggested that the Civil War might have been averted if the South had been familiar with his *Social Statics;* John Fiske asserted that his services to religion were as great as his services to science; and Henry Ward Beecher struck a rather incongruous note at the end of a hearty testimonial by promising to meet him once again beyond the grave.

However imperfect the appreciation of the guests for the niceties of Spencer's thought, the banquet showed how popular he had become in the United States. When Spencer was on the dock, waiting for the ship to carry him back to England, he seized the hands of Carnegie and Youmans. "Here," he cried to reporters, "are my two best American friends." For Spencer it was a rare gesture of personal warmth; but more than this, it symbolized the harmony of the new science with the outlook of a business civilization.

IRVIN G. WYLLIE (b. 1920), has served as chairman of the history department at the University of Wisconsin, and is now chancellor of the university's Parkside campus. Long interested in the Gilded Age businessman, Wyllie attacked the Horatio Alger belief in *The Self-Made Man in America: The Myth of Rags to Riches* (1954). He questions Hofstadter's view of the influence of Social Darwinism on the American entrepreneur on the grounds of faulty and inadmissible evidence, and suggests other ideas and beliefs which account for the mogul's views on society. Do you think Wyllie's criticisms cast doubt on Hofstadter's position?*

Irvin G. Wyllie

Alternatives to Spencerism

The American humorist Mark Twain, when asked to explain why he wore a white suit, replied that clothes make the man, that naked people have little or no influence in society. Unlike Mark Twain, or his fellow countryman Alec Guinness, Charles Darwin was no man in a white suit. But he was a man who exerted a far-reaching influence in society. If Darwin had done no more than change the methods and assumptions of the biological sciences, and contribute to the general store of scientific knowledge, he would still be an important figure in world history. The impact of his ideas was by no means limited to the sciences, however. His theory of evolution touched off a general intellectual revolution that altered the course of religious thought, redirected the social sciences, and contributed new insights and slogans to the popular and academic varieties of social theory.

The changes that flowed from the Darwinian revolution were so impressive as to suggest that it had unlimited transforming power. In the words of Bert J. Loewenberg, a pioneer student of this subject, "Evolution germinated ideas wherever it penetrated, and it penetrated everywhere." Just as historians of the American and French and Russian revolutions sometimes overestimated the extent to which these upheavals transformed the societies in which they occurred, so historians of the Darwinian intellectual

*From Irvin G. Wyllie, "Social Darwinism and the Businessman," *Proceedings of the American Philosophical Society*, vol. 103, no. 5 (1959), pp. 629–635. Footnotes omitted.

revolution have sometimes misjudged the outer limits of its influence and overestimated the completeness of its sway. The tendency to exaggerate the impact of Darwinism, especially on popular thought, is nowhere better illustrated than in the claim that American businessmen in the post-Civil War decades rationalized their personal careers and justified their business operations in terms of Herbert Spencer's competitive social version of Darwin's theory of evolution.

Even the most casual examination of American historical writing in the last twenty years reveals the prevalence of the assumption that entrepreneurs of the Gilded Age were not only practicing social Darwinists, but philosophical social Darwinists as well. Intellectual historians who treat ideas in their social contexts suggest that Darwinism served as an ideological shield and buckler for the Robber Baron generation of businessmen. In his Pulitzer prize-winning book, *The Growth of American Thought,* Merle Curti argued that defenders of rugged individualism, both inside and outside the business community, invoked Darwin to justify the struggles of the market place. Herbert Spencer became the oracle of the age, displacing Adam Smith and John Stuart Mill in the defense of *laissez faire.* In Curti's view social Darwinist doctrine "admirably suited the needs of the great captains of industry who were crushing the little fellows when these vainly tried to compete with them." In his study of *The American Mind* Henry S. Commager not only conceded the usefulness of social Darwinism to dominant business interests, but also claimed for the Spencerian system an imperial sway over the minds of most middle-class people in the half-century after Appomattox. "Between them," wrote Commager, "Dar-win and Spencer exercised such sovereignty over America as George III had never enjoyed."

Richard Hofstadter's perceptive treatise on *Social Darwinism in American Thought* offered the most systematic statement by an intellectual historian of the case for the businessman as a Darwinist. "With its rapid expansion, its exploitative methods, its desperate competition, and its peremptory rejection of failure," Hofstadter wrote, "post-bellum America was like a vast human caricature of the Darwinian struggle for existence and survival of the fittest." In this circumstance businessmen accepted Darwinian terminology "almost by instinct," and discovered that the plausible analogies of social selection were most congenial to their ways of thinking. Hofstadter quoted leading entrepreneurs, among them John D. Rockefeller, Andrew Carnegie, James J. Hill, and Chauncey Depew, to establish the Darwinian cast of their minds. Depew testified that the guests at the great banquets in New York City in the Gilded Age represented the survival of the fittest, men who had come through the fierce competitions of the great city because of their superior ability, foresight, and adaptability. James J. Hill's career in the railroad industry led him to observe that the fortunes of railroad companies were determined by the law of the survival of the fittest, a conclusion that John D. Rockefeller also allegedly reached as a result of his operations in the oil industry. When Hofstadter cited Andrew Carnegie's assertion that competition is "best for the race, because it insures the survival of the fittest in every department," this bit of evidence seemed almost superfluous in light of the case that he had already built for the captain of industry as a disciple of Herbert Spencer. . . .

Hofstadter's case, though it relies more directly on business testimony, also leaves room for doubt. Even if we were to accept all of his evidence without question, we would still be accepting a case based on the statements of only four businessmen. Part of the evidence must be questioned, however. The statement attributed to John D. Rockefeller is one he never made, namely that "The growth of a large business is merely a survival of the fittest. . . . The American beauty rose can be produced . . . only by sacrificing the early buds which grow up around it." This sentiment, uttered by John D. Rockefeller, Jr. in 1902 in an address to the YMCA at his alma mater, Brown University, may prove that the university-trained son knew how to use Darwinian phraseology, but it does not prove that his Bible-reading father was a Spencerian in the Gilded Age. Chauncey Depew's observation that the guests at the great banquets in New York represented the survival of the fittest is likewise open to objection. Since he recorded this observation in 1922, when, thanks to William Jennings Bryan, the air was filled with evolutionary discussion, we may ask how reliably this statement reflected Depew's thinking forty years before. Even if it mirrored his early thought perfectly, the fact remains that in his intellectual awareness he was no more representative of the business community than Henry Holt. A bookish man, and a Yale graduate in 1856, he was a lifelong intimate of Andrew Dixon White, the historian-president of Cornell University. He also served as a regent of the University of the State of New York from 1877 to 1904. Unlike most post-Civil War men of affairs he moved in intellectual circles, and therefore had ample opportunity to master Spencerian clichés. James J. Hill's observation that the fortunes of railroads were determined

by the law of the survival of the fittest is likewise open to the objection that a statement made in 1910 does not necessarily prove that its author took his cues from Spencer in the 1870's and 1880's. To make the case for the post-Civil War businessman as a social Darwinist we need direct testimony out of the Gilded Age.

Such testimony may be available, but so far it seems to be in short supply. In 1888 Henry Clews resorted to Darwinian analysis to explain the displacement of Wall Street's conservative old guard by a young, imaginative group of financiers after the Panic of 1857. "The change was a fine exemplification of the survival of the fittest," Clews declared, "and proved that there was a law of natural selection in financial affairs that superseded old conservatism and sealed its doom." In June of 1899 Henry O. Havemeyer, President of the American Sugar Refining Company, replied affirmatively when a member of the United States Industrial Commission asked him if he believed that a trust or combine represented the survival of the fittest in business. Havemeyer testified that he rested his whole political philosophy on this proposition. Nathan A. Taylor, an independent tin-plate manufacturer, also explained failures in his industry in terms of the survival of the fittest. If Gilded Age businessmen were social Darwinists, they could be expected to give evidence of this fact in their discussions of industrial concentration. Yet in the mountain of testimony piled up by the Congressional investigations of 1889 and 1899, talk of the survival of the fittest is exceptional, not common. And sometimes this talk originated with merchants of ideas, rather than with captains of industry. It was a newspaperman, Patrick C. Boyle of the *Oil City Derrick,* and not an official of Standard Oil, who told the United States Industrial Commission in

1899 that "Darwin's theory of survival of the fittest was never better illustrated than in the organization of the Standard Oil Company; it represents the best element in all branches of the trade."

Sometimes the direct testimony of businessmen revealed only that they were religious evolutionists, not social Darwinists. In the year 1900 the banker Roeliff Brinkerhoff reported that "I am an evolutionist of the Herbert Spencer type, and have been so from the earliest announcement of that theory, and with me it has been a power for good, and not for evil." In context Brinkerhoff's testimony indicated that evolution had influenced his religious thinking, but not his social views. In an autobiography published in the year 1885 Thomas Mellon, founder of the Mellon banking fortune, devoted fifteen pages to a discussion of evolution, all dealing with the impact of the theory on religion. He revealed himself to be a Christian and an evolutionist, but not a social Darwinist. Though Mellon believed in competition and *laissez faire*, he found his sanction in classical economics, not in Spencer's *Social Statics*.

The testimony of other businessmen before Congressional committees also revealed the persistent influence of pre-Darwinian economic ideas in the late nineteenth century. When Benjamin Brewster, president of the National Transit Company, told the House Committee on Manufactures in 1889 that there were natural laws of commerce as well as of science, he did not refer to evolution, but rather to the law of gravitation and the law of supply and demand. John E. Parsons, a trustee of the Sugar Refineries Company, invoked John Stuart Mill to defend his views in the same investigation. It was Jeremy Bentham, not Spencer, who was cited as authority for attorney John R. Dos Passos' observation to

the United States Industrial Commission that "Society is so constituted that some must suffer. It is the sacrifice that the few are forced to make for the good of the whole." Such usages require that we reconsider prevailing assumptions concerning the extent to which Herbert Spencer and William Graham Sumner displaced the classical economists as the high priests of *laissez faire*. Even more, they require that we exercise caution in attributing to Darwin and Spencer ultimate responsibility for the competitive social ideas of the businessman in the Gilded Age.

Too often, after an uncooperative captain of industry has refused to identify himself as a social Darwinist, he has been asked to step down from the witness stand, so that a sociologist or economist might take his place. Richard Hofstadter, convinced that businessmen "are not the most articulate social philosophers," called upon a reform-minded University of Chicago sociologist, Charles R. Henderson, to testify to the Darwinian cast of the entrepreneurial mind. "It would be strange if the 'captain of industry' did not sometimes manifest a militant spirit," Henderson wrote in 1896, "for he has risen from the ranks largely because he was a better fighter than most of us. Competitive commercial life is not a flower bed of ease, but a battle field where the 'struggle for existence' is defining the industrially fittest to survive." All this statement proved was that Henderson, an intellectual, had the ability to see Darwinian meaning in the struggles of the business world. He did not pretend that the businessman saw his activities in the same light. In fact he deplored the ideological gulf that separated the entrepreneur from the social theorist, and acknowledged that businessmen did not hold the intellectual in high esteem. "They say, with some touch of contemptuous sarcasm and cynicism," Henderson wrote, "that they can hire talkers and buy books."

Gilded Age businessmen were not sufficiently bookish, or sufficiently well educated, to keep up with the changing world of ideas. As late as 1900, 84 per cent of the businessmen listed in *Who's Who in America* had not been educated beyond high school. Though college men in business increased steadily in the last decades of the nineteenth century, they were always a minority. The uneducated majority had little time for books. Cornelius Vanderbilt, who read only one book in his life, *Pilgrim's Progress,* after he was seventy years of age, once remarked that if he had taken time to learn education he would not have had time to learn anything else. Many an unlettered businessman undoubtedly shared this view, and also subscribed to Daniel Drew's opinion that "Book learning is something, but thirteen million dollars is also something, and a mighty sight more." Since in the late nineteenth century Darwin's adherents were for the most part scientists, social scientists, philosophers, clergymen, editors, and other educationally advantaged persons, it would be surprising to find a really large contingent of businessmen in his camp. The minority of college graduates and devotees of self-culture may be found there, but the untutored majority probably will not.

Scholars whose work requires them to deal with ideas in a systematic way, and to keep abreast of changing modes of thought, are generally reluctant to concede that other men may be far behind the times, and philosophically disorganized and inconsistent as well. To them it is unthinkable that any influential body of men in the Gilded Age should have failed to embrace the most advanced idea of that age, and that businessmen in particular could have ignored a formulation like that of Spencer, which seemed to explain so many hard facts of business life. However, there is considerable wisdom in the observation that "It must not be thought that Social Darwinism made brutal misanthropists of the Great Entrepreneurs and the Finance Capitalists. They were, by and large, too simple-minded for that; it was only an intellectual like W. G. Sumner who became a misanthropist." Though John D. Rockefeller might transact business according to the law of the jungle, he was a pious Christian who looked upon his wealth as a God-given reward for virtue. Railroad executives, who by certain reckonings were social Darwinists, sometimes violated Spencerian efficiency by decreeing that in slack times single men should be fired first, to be followed by men with the least seniority. Andrew Carnegie, a secular-minded man and a tough-minded Darwinian, was also a generous philanthropist who gave a practical demonstration of the social utility of the old Christian doctrine of the stewardship of wealth. Robert Harris, whose job as president of the Chicago, Burlington, and Quincy Railroad might have been expected to put him on the side of the survival of the fittest, testified that "As a general proposition, it seems to me that the strong should help the weak, now by one course and now by another; and in exercising authority to do it as we would wish it done to ourselves."

Anyone who examines the voluminous nineteenth-century literature of business success cannot fail to be impressed that businessmen who talked about success and failure took their texts from Christian moralists, not from Darwin and Spencer. In the race for wealth they attributed little influence to native intelligence, physical strength, or any other endowment of nature, and paramount influence to industry, frugality, and sobriety — simple moral virtues that any man could cultivate. They urged young men to seek the business way of life in the Bible, not in *The Descent of Man* or *The Principles of Sociology*. The problem of success was not that of grinding down one's competitors, but of elevating one's self — and the two were not equivalent. Business practice may have suggested a Darwinian struggle for existence, but self-help advisers of the Gilded Age suggested that the only struggle of consequence was the struggle for good character. Failure was likewise attributed to defective character rather than to deficiencies of endowment or opportunity. Opportunities for success, like opportunities for salvation, were limitless; heaven could receive as many as were worthy. Because American businessmen operated in a land blessed with an abundance of resources they rejected the Malthusian idea that chances were so limited that one man's rise meant the fall of many others. Theirs was a more optimistic view, that every triumph opened the way for more. Advanced thinkers might explain both success and failure in terms of social Darwinism, but most businessmen were probably inclined to follow the lead of the *Commercial and Financial Chronicle* in permitting "this fashionable philosophy . . . to spin its shining web and to apply its specious theories where it can."

In order to deprive the captain of industry of the public relations advantage he enjoyed when he passed himself off as a model of virtue, critics of business in the late nineteenth and early twentieth centuries represented that the great barons were robber barons who knew no moral law except that of the jungle. They inverted the businessman's moral pyra-

mid and tried to demonstrate that he owed his success not to simple Christian virtues, but to brutality, rapacity, dishonesty, and cunning. Augustus Tack, a petroleum refiner who had been squeezed out by Standard Oil, gained a measure of revenge in 1889 when he described Rockefeller as a heartless Darwinist to the House Committee on Manufactures. Tack testified that he had gone to Rockefeller, hoping for a reprieve, but that he had been sent away with the brutal comment, "There is no hope. . . . The weakest must go first." Henry Demarest Lloyd, that erstwhile critic of Rockefeller and student of Standard Oil, observed in *Wealth Against Commonwealth* that "The man who should apply in his family or his citizenship this 'survival of the fittest theory' as it is practically professed and operated in business would be a monster, and would be speedily made extinct, as we do with monsters." When John D. Rockefeller, Jr. made his unfortunate remarks about the American Beauty rose in 1902 he discovered that he had played into the hands of his father's enemies as well as his own. Critics who denounced him as "a young scion of wealth and greed, possessed of more dollars than ideas," forgot that the title of his talk had been "Christianity in Business," and that he had entered a plea for more Christian virtue in the transaction of business. In the spring of 1905, at the height of the "tainted money" controversy, his father's enemies depicted the senior Rockefeller, pruning shears in hand, cutting away the buds that had grown up around the finest flower of the oil industry.

Rockefeller was not the only businessman to be tarred with the brush of social Darwinism in the era of the muckrakers. In his criticism of the men who organized the Beef Trust, Charles Edward Russell explained that "They have merely followed to its logical conclusion the idea of the survival of the fittest, the right of the strong to annihilate the weak, the theory that in business any advantage is fair—the accepted creed of inordinate gain." All the leading muckrakers sensed that there was no better way to discredit a businessman than to portray him as a renegade of the jungle. In light of the eagerness of early twentieth-century critics to condemn the entrepreneur as a Spencerian, it is ironic that sympathetic students of business in our own time have tried so hard to link the businessman to social Darwinism.

THORSTEIN VEBLEN (1857–1929), one of the great economic minds of modern times, challenged the ideas of classical theoreticians by weaving history and sociology into what came to be known as "institutional" economics. Eccentric in his habits, Veblen taught at several leading universities and finally retired to a cabin in California. In addition to his best-known work, *The Theory of the Leisure Class* (1899), he wrote *The Theory of Business Enterprise* (1904), *Absentee Ownership and Business Enterprise* (1923), and *The Engineers and the Price System* (1921). Equipped with a wide-ranging wit, Veblen writes of the leisure class with a satire marked by deadly seriousness. Coining the term conspicuous consumption, he assails the mogul's ostentatious living with regard to utilitarian goods, such as houses and even spoons, as the worship and pursuit of a meaningless value system. Should the robber baron have sought alternative uses for his great wealth?*

Thorstein Veblen

The Folly of Conspicuous Consumption

The caution has already been repeated more than once, that while the regulating norm of consumption is in large part the requirement of conspicuous waste, it must not be understood that the motive on which the consumer acts in any given case is this principle in its bald, unsophisticated form. Ordinarily his motive is a wish to conform to established usage, to avoid unfavorable notice and comment, to live up to the accepted canons of decency in the kind, amount, and grade of goods consumed, as well as in the decorous employment of his time and effort. In the common run of cases this sense of prescriptive usage is present in the motives of the consumer and exerts a direct constraining force, especially as regards consumption carried on under the eyes of observers. But a considerable element of prescriptive expensiveness is observable also in consumption that does not in any appreciable degree become known to outsiders—as, for instance, articles of underclothing, some articles of food, kitchen utensils, and other household apparatus designed for service rather than for evidence. In all such useful articles a close scrutiny will discover certain features which add to the cost and enhance the commercial value of the goods in question, but do not proportionately increase the serviceability of these articles for the material purposes which alone they ostensibly are designed to serve.

*From Thorstein Veblen, *The Theory of the Leisure Class* (New York: The Macmillan Company, 1899, 1912), pp. 115–116, 119–122, 126–133, 153–154, 348–350.

Under the selective surveillance of the law of conspicuous waste there grows up a code of accredited canons of consumption, the effect of which is to hold the consumer up to a standard of expensiveness and wastefulness in his consumption of goods and in his employment of time and effort. This growth of prescriptive usage has an immediate effect upon economic life, but it has also an indirect and remoter effect upon conduct in other respects as well. Habits of thought with respect to the expression of life in any given direction unavoidably affect the habitual view of what is good and right in life in other directions also. In the organic complex of habits of thought which make up the substance of an individual's conscious life the economic interest does not lie isolated and distinct from all other interests. Something, for instance, has already been said of its relation to the canons of reputability. . . .

Obviously, the canon of conspicuous waste is accountable for a great portion of what may be called devout consumption; as, *e.g.,* the consumption of sacred edifices, vestments, and other goods of the same class. Even in those modern cults to whose divinities is imputed a predilection for temples not built with hands, the sacred buildings and the other properties of the cult are constructed and decorated with some view to a reputable degree of wasteful expenditure. And it needs but little either of observation or introspection—and either will serve the turn—to assure us that the expensive splendor of the house of worship has an appreciable uplifting and mellowing effect upon the worshipper's frame of mind. It will serve to enforce the same fact if we reflect upon the sense of abject shamefulness with which any evidence of indigence or squalor about the sacred place affects all beholders. The acces-

sories of any devout observance should be pecuniarily above reproach. This requirement is imperative, whatever latitude may be allowed with regard to these accessories in point of aesthetic or other serviceability.

It may also be in place to notice that in all communities, especially in neighborhoods where the standard of pecuniary decency for dwellings is not high, the local sanctuary is more ornate, more conspicuously wasteful in its architecture and decoration, than the dwelling houses of the congregation. This is true of nearly all denominations and cults, whether Christian or Pagan, but it is true in a peculiar degree of the older and maturer cults. At the same time the sanctuary commonly contributes little if anything to the physical comfort of the members. Indeed, the sacred structure not only serves the physical well-being of the members to but a slight extent, as compared with their humbler dwelling-houses; but it is felt by all men that a right and enlightened sense of the true, the beautiful, and the good demands that in all expenditure on the sanctuary anything that might serve the comfort of the worshipper should be conspicuously absent. If any element of comfort is admitted in the fittings of the sanctuary, it should be at least scrupulously screened and masked under an ostensible austerity. In the most reputable latter-day houses of worship, where no expense is spared, the principle of austerity is carried to the length of making the fittings of the place a means of mortifying the flesh, especially in appearance. There are few persons of delicate tastes in the matter of devout consumption to whom this austerely wasteful discomfort does not appeal as intrinsically right and good. Devout consumption is of the nature of vicarious consumption. This canon of devout austerity is based on the pecuniary reputability of conspicuously wasteful consumption, backed by the principle that vicarious consumption should conspicuously not conduce to the comfort of the vicarious consumer.

The sanctuary and its fittings have something of this austerity in all the cults in which the saint or divinity to whom the sanctuary pertains is not conceived to be present and make personal use of the property for the gratification of luxurious tastes imputed to him. The character of the sacred paraphernalia is somewhat different in this respect in those cults where the habits of life imputed to the divinity more nearly approach those of an earthly patriarchal potentate—where he is conceived to make use of these consumable goods in person. In the latter case the sanctuary and its fittings take on more of the fashion given to goods destined for the conspicuous consumption of a temporal master or owner. On the other hand, where the sacred apparatus is simply employed in the divinity's service, that is to say, where it is consumed vicariously on his account by his servants, there the sacred properties take the character suited to goods that are destined for vicarious consumption only.

In the latter case the sanctuary and the sacred apparatus are so contrived as not to enhance the comfort or fullness of life of the vicarious consumer, or at any rate not to convey the impression that the end of their consumption is the consumer's comfort. For the end of vicarious consumption is to enhance, not the fullness of life of the consumer, but the pecuniary repute of the master for whose behoof the consumption takes place. Therefore priestly vestments are notoriously expensive, ornate, and inconvenient; and in the cults where the priestly servitor of the divinity is not conceived to serve him in the capacity of consort, they are of an austere, comfortless fashion. And such it is felt that they should be. . . .

These canons of reputability have had a similar, but more far-reaching and more specifically determinable, effect upon the popular sense of beauty or serviceability in consumable goods. The requirements of pecuniary decency have, to a very appreciable extent, influenced the sense of beauty and of utility in articles of use or beauty. Articles are to an extent preferred for use on account of their being conspicuously wasteful; they are felt to be serviceable somewhat in proportion as they are wasteful and ill adapted to their ostensible use.

The utility of articles valued for their beauty depends closely upon the expensiveness of the articles. A homely illustration will bring out this dependence. A hand-wrought silver spoon, of a commercial value of some ten to twenty dollars, is not ordinarily more serviceable—in the first sense of the word—than a machine-made spoon of the same material. It may not even be more serviceable than a machine-made spoon of some "base" metal, such as aluminum, the value of which may be no more than some ten to twenty cents. The former of the two utensils is, in fact, commonly a less effective contrivance for its ostensible purpose than the latter. The objection is of course ready to hand that, in taking this view of the matter, one of the chief uses, if not the chief use, of the costlier spoon is ignored; the hand-wrought spoon gratifies our taste, our sense of the beautiful, while that made by machinery out of the base metal has no useful office beyond a brute efficiency. The facts are no doubt as the objection states them, but it will be evident on reflection that the objection is after all more plausible than conclusive. It appears (1) that while the different materials of which the two spoons are made each possesses beauty and serviceability for the purpose for which it is used, the material of the hand-wrought spoon is some one hundred times more valuable than the baser metal, without very greatly excelling the latter in intrinsic beauty of grain or color, and without being in any appreciable degree superior in point of mechanical serviceability; (2) if a close inspection should show that the supposed hand-wrought spoon were in reality only a very clever imitation of hand-wrought goods, but an imitation so cleverly wrought as to give the same impression of line and surface to any but a minute examination by a trained eye, the utility of the article, including the gratification which the user derives from its contemplation as an object of beauty, would immediately decline by some eighty or ninety per cent, or even more; (3) if the two spoons are, to a fairly close observer, so nearly identical in appearance that the lighter weight of the spurious article alone betrays it, this identity of form and color will scarcely add to the value of the machine-made spoon, nor appreciably enhance the gratification of the user's "sense of beauty" in contemplating it, so long as the cheaper spoon is not a novelty, and so long as it can be procured at a nominal cost.

The case of the spoons is typical. The superior gratification derived from the use and contemplation of costly and supposedly beautiful products is, commonly, in great measure a gratification of our sense of costliness masquerading under the name of beauty. Our higher appreciation of the superior article is an appreciation of its superior honorific character, much more frequently than it is an unsophisticated appreciation of its beauty. The requirement of conspicuous wastefulness is not commonly present, consciously, in our canons of taste, but it is none

the less present as a constraining norm selectively shaping and sustaining our sense of what is beautiful, and guiding our discrimination with respect to what may legitimately be approved as beautiful and what may not.

It is at this point, where the beautiful and the honorific meet and blend, that a discrimination between serviceability and wastefulness is most difficult in any concrete case. It frequently happens that an article which serves the honorific purpose of conspicuous waste is at the same time a beautiful object; and the same application of labor to which it owes its utility for the former purpose may, and often does, give beauty of form and color to the article. The question is further complicated by the fact that many objects, as, for instance, the precious stones and the metals and some other materials used for adornment and decoration, owe their utility as items of conspicuous waste to an antecedent utility as objects of beauty. Gold, for instance, has a high degree of sensuous beauty; very many if not most of the highly prized works of art are intrinsically beautiful, though often with material qualification; the like is true of some stuffs used for clothing, of some landscapes, and of many other things in less degree. Except for this intrinsic beauty which they possess, these objects would scarcely have been coveted as they are, or have become monopolized objects of pride to their possessors and users. But the utility of these things to the possessor is commonly due less to their intrinsic beauty than to the honor which their possession and consumption confers, or to the obloquy which it wards off.

Apart from their serviceability in other respects, these objects are beautiful and have a utility as such; they are valuable on this account if they can be appropriated or monopolized; they are, therefore, coveted as valuable possessions, and their exclusive enjoyment gratifies the possessor's sense of pecuniary superiority at the same time that their contemplation gratifies his sense of beauty. But their beauty, in the naïve sense of the word, is the occasion rather than the ground of their monopolization or of their commerical value. "Great as is the sensuous beauty of gems, their rarity and price adds an expression of distinction to them, which they would never have if they were cheap." There is, indeed, in the common run of cases under this head, relatively little incentive to the exclusive possession and use of these beautiful things, except on the ground of their honorific character as items of conspicuous waste. Most objects of this general class, with the partial exception of articles of personal adornment, would serve all other purposes than the honorific one equally well, whether owned by the person viewing them or not; and even as regards personal ornaments it is to be added that their chief purpose is to lend éclat to the person of their wearer (or owner) by comparison with other persons who are compelled to do without. The aesthetic serviceability of objects of beauty is not greatly nor universally heightened by possession.

The generalization for which the discussion so far affords ground is that any valuable object in order to appeal to our sense of beauty must conform to the requirements of beauty and of expensiveness both. But this is not all. Beyond this the canon of expensiveness also affects our tastes in such a way as to inextricably blend the marks of expensiveness, in our appreciation, with the beautiful features of the object, and to subsume the resultant effect under the head of an appreciation of beauty simply. The marks of expensiveness come to be accepted as beautiful

features of the expensive articles. They are pleasing as being marks of honorific costliness, and the pleasure which they afford on this score blends with that afforded by the beautiful form and color of the object; so that we often declare that an article of apparel, for instance, is "perfectly lovely," when pretty much all that an analysis of the aesthetic value of the article would leave ground for is the declaration that it is pecuniarily honorific.

This blending and confusion of the elements of expensiveness and of beauty is, perhaps, best exemplified in articles of dress and of household furniture. The code of reputability in matters of dress decides what shapes, colors, materials, and general effects in human apparel are for the time to be accepted as suitable; and departures from the code are offensive to our taste, supposedly as being departures from aesthetic truth. The approval with which we look upon fashionable attire is by no means to be accounted pure make-believe. We readily, and for the most part with utter sincerity, find those things pleasing that are in vogue. Shaggy dress-stuffs and pronounced color effects, for instance, offend us at times when the vogue is goods of a high, glossy finish and neutral colors. A fancy bonnet of this year's model unquestionably appeals to our sensibilities today much more forcibly than an equally fancy bonnet of the model of last year; although when viewed in the perspective of a quarter of a century, it would, I apprehend, be a matter of the utmost difficulty to award the palm for intrinsic beauty to the one rather than to the other of these structures. So, again, it may be remarked that, considered simply in their physical juxtaposition with the human form, the high gloss of a gentleman's hat or of a patent-leather shoe has no more of intrinsic beauty than a similarly high gloss on a threadbare sleeve; and yet there is no question but that all well-bred people (in the Occidental civilized communities) instinctively and unaffectedly cleave to the one as a phenomenon of great beauty, and eschew the other as offensive to every sense to which it can appeal. It is extremely doubtful if any one could be induced to wear such a contrivance as the high hat of civilized society, except for some urgent reason based on other than aesthetic grounds.

By further habituation to an appreciative perception of the marks of expensiveness in goods, and by habitually identifying beauty with reputability, it comes about that a beautiful article which is not expensive is accounted not beautiful. In this way it has happened, for instance, that some beautiful flowers pass conventionally for offensive weeds; others that can be cultivated with relative ease are accepted and admired by the lower middle class, who can afford no more expensive luxuries of this kind; but these varieties are rejected as vulgar by those people who are better able to pay for expensive flowers and who are educated to a higher schedule of pecuniary beauty in the florist's products; while still other flowers, of no greater intrinsic beauty than these, are cultivated at great cost and call out much admiration from flower-lovers whose tastes have been matured under the critical guidance of a polite environment.

The same variation in matters of taste, from one class of society to another, is visible also as regards many other kinds of consumable goods, as, for example, is the case with furniture, houses, parks, and gardens. This diversity of views as to what is beautiful in these various classes of goods is not a diversity of the norm according to which the unsophisticated sense of the beautiful works. It is not a constitutional difference of endowments in the aesthetic respect, but rather a difference in the code of reputability which specifies what objects properly lie within the scope of honorific consumption for the class to which the critic belongs. It is a difference in the traditions of propriety with respect to the kinds of things which may, without derogation to the consumer, be consumed under the head of objects of taste and art. With a certain allowance for variations to be accounted for on other grounds, these traditions are determined, more or less rigidly, by the pecuniary plane of life of the class. . . .

This process of selective adaptation of designs to the end of conspicuous waste, and the substitution of pecuniary beauty for aesthetic beauty, has been especially effective in the development of architecture. It would be extremely difficult to find a modern civilized residence or public building which can claim anything better than relative inoffensiveness in the eyes of anyone who will dissociate the elements of beauty from those of honorific waste. The endless variety of fronts presented by the better class of tenements and apartment houses in our cities is an endless variety of architectural distress and of suggestions of expensive discomfort. Considered as objects of beauty, the dead walls of the sides and back of these structures, left untouched by the hands of the artist, are commonly the best feature of the building. . .

What is true of the efficiency of organizations for non-invidious work in this respect is true also as regards the work of individuals proceeding on the same motives; though it perhaps holds true with more qualification for individuals than for organized enterprises. The habit of gauging merit by the leisure-class canons of wasteful expenditure and unfamiliarity with vulgar life, whether on the side of production or of consumption, is necessarily strong in the individuals who aspire to do some work of public utility. And if the individual should forget his station and turn his efforts to vulgar effectiveness, the common sense of the community—the sense of pecuniary decency—would presently reject his work and set him right. An example of this is seen in the administration of bequests made by public-spirited men for the single purpose (at least ostensibly) of furthering the facility of human life in some particular respect. The objects for which bequests of this class are most frequently made at present are schools, libraries, hospitals, and asylums for the infirm or unfortunate. The avowed purpose of the donor in these cases is the amelioration of human life in the particular respect which is named in the bequest; but it will be found an invariable rule that in the execution of the work not a little of other motives, frequently incompatible with the initial motive, is present and determines the particular disposition eventually made of a good share of the means which have been set apart by the bequest. Certain funds, for instance, may have been set apart as a foundation for a foundling asylum or a retreat for invalids. The diversion of expenditure to honorific waste in such cases is not uncommon enough to cause surprise or even to raise a smile. An appreciable share of the funds is spent in the construction of an edifice faced with some aesthetically objectionable but expensive stone, covered with grotesque and incongruous details, and designed, in its battlemented walls and turrets and its massive portals and strategic approaches, to suggest certain barbaric methods of warfare. The interior of the structure shows the same pervasive guidance of the canons of conspicuous waste and predatory exploit, The windows, for instance, to go no farther into detail, are placed with a view to impress their pecuniary excellence upon the chance beholder from the outside, rather than with a view to effectiveness for their ostensible end in the convenience or comfort of the beneficiaries within; and the detail of interior arrangement is required to conform itself as best it may to this alien but imperious requirement of pecuniary beauty.

In all this, of course, it is not to be presumed that the donor would have found fault, or that he would have done otherwise if he had taken control in person; it appears that in those cases where such a personal direction is exercised—where the enterprise is conducted by direct expenditure and superintendence instead of by bequest—the aims and methods of management are not different in this respect. Nor would the beneficiaries, or the outside observers whose ease or vanity are not immediately touched, be pleased with a different disposition of the funds. It would suit no one to have the enterprise conducted with a view directly to the most economical and effective use of the means at hand for the initial, material end of the foundation. All concerned, whether their interest is immediate and self-regarding, or contemplative only, agree that some considerable share of the expenditure should go to the higher or spiritual needs derived from the habit of an invidious comparison in predatory exploit and pecuniary waste. But this only goes to say that the canons of emulative and pecuniary reputability so far pervade the common sense of the community as to permit no escape or evasion, even in the case of an enterprise which ostensibly proceeds entirely on the basis of a noninvidious interest.

EDWARD CHASE KIRKLAND (b. 1894), is currently
the leading defender of the businessman among
historians. Now professor emeritus at Bowdoin College,
Kirkland first established his reputation in 1932 with
an economic history textbook, which has undergone
several revisions. In addition to the work in which
this passage appears, he has contributed such
outstanding studies as *Men, Cities, and Transportation:
A Study in New England History* (1948), *Business in
the Gilded Age: The Conservatives' Balance Sheet*
(1952), and *Industry Comes of Age: Business, Labor,
and Public Policy 1860–1897* (1961). Is Kirkland
correct when he dismisses Veblen's explanation of
"conspicious consumption" as too simple? And are his
several explanations of the "big house" enough to
absolve the mogul of total guilt?*

Edward Chase Kirkland

The Big House Revisited

Why did they do it? Why did the business leaders from San Francisco to Bar
Harbor have to live in houses with libraries, billiard rooms, art galleries,
several rooms in which to eat, at least
one of which had to be two stories high
and paneled to the ceiling, buildings
sometimes equipped with small theatres
and perhaps even a chapel capable of
holding a considerable congregation?
There is an assumption here made by
most critics that the owners of the houses
conceived of them and wanted them. The
antibusiness critics found this an accept-
able explanation, and so did the architects who were prone to assume a wearied
and frustrated air after their bouts with
the tastes and budgets of their patrons.

But the architects themselves may have
been largely responsible for the extravagance of these edifices. An art dealer,
like Duveen, sharpened the appetites of
millionaires for fine art as well as instructed their tastes. Architects, rewarded
by percentage commissions, and the
larger the cost the higher the commission,
performed the same function when it
came to housing millionaires.

The conventional explanation for the
big house has been that the robber baron,
like his prototype abroad, demanded in
his housing: bulk, space, and permanence.
This hankering was almost a matter of
the genes. This biological link between
wealth and houses has been analyzed with
somewhat more acumen as well as per-

*Reprinted from Edward Chase Kirkland: *Dream and Thought in the Business Community*, 1860–1900.
© 1956 by Cornell University. Used by permission of Cornell University Press. Pp. 33–49. Footnotes omitted.

suasiveness by Thorstein Veblen in his *Theory of the Leisure Class*. Though he does not bear down upon housing in that essay, Veblen advances as explanation for architectural extravagance that in a pecuniary culture the leisure class, for example, the businessman, demonstrated its honorific position by conspicuous leisure. As the opportunities for display through this channel shrink, the group resorts increasingly to conspicuous and unnecessary consumption. Big houses, like wasteful food and drink and sport and a classical education, are in this category. Certainly the conception of the big house as a sort of visible bank balance fits in neatly with many contemporary developments, and accords with the persistent tendency to exaggerate the cost of the millionaire's mansion. Thus Marshall Field's house in Chicago was "said to have cost two million dollars"; the actual cost of house, furniture, stables, and horses was, according to a memorandum in the Field papers, about $175,000. If the purpose was display, imprecision of this sort is a positive advantage.

Like many generalizations, Veblen's was too simple. The motives for the big house were complex. Sometimes wives drove husbands to these expenditures; sometimes husbands undertook them as a gesture of romance to their wives. The newly rich who once, like as not, had lived in cramped quarters and as children slept several to a room, if not a bed, were now willing to pay handsomely for space and privacy. Nor was the chance to invest in a sound property or convert a poor one into a paying proposition lacking, as Potter Palmer and Mark Hopkins and others demonstrated. However impelling such motivations for action, they were hardly usable as a rationale for the big house. Since all expenditure employed labor, the construction and maintenance

of the big house made work; this was commendable. Thus Edward Atkinson in 1886 informed a group of Providence workingmen that Mr. Vanderbilt

built a most expensive dwelling-house, of which he occupied a part, his servants obtaining their shelter in the other part. . . . Such a dwelling is not capital. That is to say, it produces nothing. . . . It may be very foolish for the owner of capital, or of that which might become capital, . . . to spend it on fancy farms, palatial dwellings, or things of that sort; but in such expenditure he gives employment for that period during which the expenditure is being made to a very large number of persons.

The big house distributes money:

although it may not be the wisest method, it is the only method consistent with the present standard of education and opportunity. . . . I do not myself justify many of these lavish expenditures. I think that a man, however rich he may be, is very foolish to build a dwelling-house, which must be sold either by his children or his grandchildren, for the reason that none of them can afford to live in it under the righteous method of distributing property, which prevails in this country.

Whether satirizing the Boston calculator or not, Mr. Dooley was cautioning his Hennessy:

Now, don't go gettin' cross about th' rich, Hinnissy. Put up that dinnymite. Don't excite ye'ersilf about us folks in Newport. It's always been th' same way, Father Kelly tells me. Says he: "If a man is wise, he gets rich an' if he gets rich, he gets foolish, or his wife does. That's what keeps the money movin' around. What comes in at th' ticker goes out at the wine agent. F'river an' iver people have been growin' rich, goin' down to some kind iv a Newport, makin' monkeys iv thimsilves an' goin' back to the jungle. . . . An' . . . I'm glad there is a Newport," he says. "It's th' exhaust pipe," he says. "Without it we might blow up," he says. "It's th' hole in th' top iv th' kettle," he says. "I wish it was bigger."

A genuine Protestant minister, rather than a supposititious Catholic priest, preached the same doctrine. William H. P. Faunce, onetime Rockefeller's pastor and later president of Brown University, declared in 1893: "The man who possesses a fortune is *nolens volens* a benefactor to the community. He may be a misanthrope and atheist. But if such a man moves into a western city and begins to spend his money in the most selfish and ostentatious luxury, he is an involuntary benefactor of that city." In addition to employing labor the expenditures of rich men went for the support of art; wealth had been historically the latter's patron. Ornamentation and decoration were possible in a chateau, impossible in a cottage. The big house adorned and beautified the community. It was a matter of civic pride. This was another justification for the private palace.

Defenses from expediency were probably more persuasive than the argument from right. Henry George made it clear that in his philosophy the rich man with money could do as he wanted with it. "If he gets his wealth without robbing anybody else, without preventing anybody else from having *his* fair opportunity to produce wealth, we can safely leave it to him and let him put up a pyramid with it, or make a big bonfire of it, or throw it into the sea, if he desires." Indeed, some commentators held that the failure of the capitalist to build a big house was an indictment of selfishness and greed. It was an obligation of the rich to live lavishly. Ida M. Tarbell, in a *McClure's Magazine* article in 1905, discharged against John D. Rockefeller all the buckshot she had not been able to use in her *History of the Standard Oil Company*. One of her accusations was the unpretentiousness of Rockefeller's homes.

No one of the three houses he occupies has any claims to rank among the notable homes of the country. . . . They show him to have no pleasure in noble architecture, to appreciate nothing of the beauty of fine lines and decorations. Mr. Rockefeller's favorite home, the house at Forest Hill, is a monument of cheap ugliness.

In short, he was no "splendid old Venetian" who liked to squander his fortune on palaces and galleries—"so far as the world knows, he is poor in his pleasures." In sum, here was the "money-mad" miser. Reflecting upon these and other paradoxes, E. L. Godkin came to the conclusion that the display expenditures of the rich were "in a certain sense, the product of the popular manners."

Squinting at European precedents with which he was acquainted, Godkin feared that American rich men in building great houses—"slavish imitation"—were making two radical mistakes. Overseas the possession of big houses had as its "reasons"—the ownership of great territorial possessions and "the practice of hospitality on a scale unknown among us." The owner gathers about him "a large circle of men and women . . . who can talk to each other so as to entertain each other about sport, or art, or literature, or politics," particularly over week ends. In America these precedent conditions were lacking. The owner of the big house might collect people in his drawing room.

But what kind of company would it be? How many of the guests would have anything to say to each other? Suppose "stocks" to be ruled out, where would the topics of conversation be found? Would there be much to talk about except the size of the host's fortune, and that of some other persons present? How many of the men would wish to sit with the ladies in the evening and participate with them in conversation? Would the host attempt two such gatherings, without abandoning his efforts in disgust, selling out the whole concern, and going to Europe?

In spite of its sharpness, this was criticism on a charitable and kindly plane. Much more common was the charge that the big house was not necessary; it was "luxury." Luxurious living was bad, first of all, for those who lived in such a manner. Such houses contributed to "the high tension of life; the temptations it thus opens to business men, goaded to speculation and peculation to keep up with the 'style'; the stimulus it gives to the idle and frivolous and sensuous life of women (and sensuous is not far from sensual)," declared an Episcopalian minister, spokesman for the social gospel. Ludwig Lewisohn in his discussion of Howells' *Rise of Silas Lapham* has observed that in that generation a girl's room "seemed terribly intimate. . . . Irene blushed deeply and turned her head away" when her father mentioned it. A house with forty bedrooms could not be pure. Inferences of this sort received factual support from Jim Fisk, who along with Gould purchased a marble palace in mid-town New York. This they converted into offices for the Erie Railroad. The palace also contained an opera house. As Henry Adams observed, "The atmosphere of the Erie offices was not supposed to be disturbed with moral prejudices; and as the opera itself supplied Mr. Fisk's mind with amusement, so the opera *troupe* supplied him with a permanent harem. Whatever Mr. Fisk did was done on an extraordinary scale." We need not take this example too seriously. Fisk was not typical, for, according to James Ford Rhodes, the historian, business to Fisk "seemed to be a joke." Large houses required paintings; these might make matters much worse. An "estimable family"

might even propose "to decorate a dining-room ceiling with a copy of the paintings to which the *demi-monde* look up in a celebrated café of Paris." Commodore Vanderbilt's son might outrage the public's notion of railroad responsibility by incautiously saying, "The public be damned," but he took precaution not to give offense in terms of art patronage. The Awakening of Aurora on his wife's bedroom ceiling was not "questionable" since "this imaginative rendering is expressed in figures . . . from which every trace of the empire of carnal sense has been kept away."

In addition to setting a bad example, big houses were also likely to arouse social discontent. Certainly this was not the purpose of their owners, for the houses were not built to impress the groundlings. Chateau row along Fifth Avenue appeared long before the rubberneck busses proceeded up the thoroughfare while the barker's megaphone informed passengers choked by exhaust smoke and carbon monoxide of the accumulated wealth there on display; nor were the cable cars on Nob Hill then built to carry the curious to the summit where they could gape at the castles of railroad and mining kings. Furthermore Newport and Asheville, comparatively speaking, could muster no crowds to gaze at palaces. These palaces were erected to impress one's fellow millionaires. Nonetheless the contrast was there. The young Gifford Pinchot, employed to his delight as a forester on Vanderbilt's Biltmore estate, meditated upon the chateau: "As a feudal castle it would have been beyond criticism, and perhaps beyond praise. But in the United States of the nineteenth century and among the one-room cabins of the Appalachian mountaineers, it did not belong. The contrast was a devastating commentary on the injustice of concentrated wealth." Of course in the burgeoning urban areas the contrast was sharper. The millionaire's palace was at one end of the avenue; the overcrowded tenement at the other. Even the stables of the former cost more and were more comfortable than the latter.

Still it was hard to answer the argument that the construction of the big house employed labor and, by chance, provided patronage for the arts. American architects were backward in providing a counter rationale. Discriminating students of architecture, like Russell Sturgis, Jr., might deliver an occasional obiter dictum to the effect that "ostentation," "mere glitter," and "mere display of costliness" were not avenues to art, but the apostles of the newness in American architecture, in spite of their frequent and loud pronouncements in favor of democracy and the people, rarely provided social criticism of the big house. Louis Sullivan's mirth at the chateau that Richard M. Hunt provided for W. K. Vanderbilt on Fifth Avenue was scorn at the chronological inappropriateness of such a building for a "gentleman in a silk hat." Perhaps English critics would make good the deficiency. John Ruskin and William Morris, it was said, had demonstrated that art came out of the people. "Art was not born in the palace; rather she fell sick there, and it will take more bracing air than that of rich men's houses to heal her again." A sound art could arise only from a sound society. And luxury, equivalent to frivolity or selfishness, could not provide a fit environment for "the highest art." That the construction of the big house provided jobs was a "sophistry," that it had aesthetic byproducts might be demonstrated, but Americans needed

"genuine aestheticism and not the 'Oscar Wilde' sort."

Actually when struck, allies, like Morris and Ruskin, gave back an uncertain sound. Ruskin advocated no "meanness of private habitation. I would fain introduce into it all magnificence, care, and beauty, where they are possible; but I would not have that *useless* expense in *unnoticed* fineries or formalities." (Italics mine.) William Morris detected the Philistine among all classes and pitied the rich men, who by their failure to rise above the "brutality" of the masses "had defrauded themselves as well as the poor," and commended the expenditures of the rich as long as their motives were good. Costliness "is not luxury, if it be done for beauty's sake, and not for show." In view of the contradictions of these English prophets, the impatience of Senator Blair of New Hampshire, chairman of the Senate Committee on Education and Labor, with a witness who claimed Ruskin "has given the best definition of money of any man living" was understandable. Blair replied, "Mr. Ruskin is a fine painter."

In the end, the American attack on the big house fell back upon terms of expediency and morality. On the first count, people of that day were prone to worry about what they called "the dangerous classes." It was said such were more likely to be found in the "private palace" than in the "pestiferous tenement." As for morality, it was wrong for rich men to spend so much money on extravagant housing. Occasionally implicit in this argument was the idea that the money would be better spent for other purposes, perhaps model housing for the poor or some other humanitarian enterprise. "One gorgeous palace absorbs all the labor and expense that might have made a thousand hovels comfortable." So if the millionaire had already demonstrated a philanthropic tendency, he could be forgiven an indulgence in the big house. "Who ever would have grudged dear old Peter Cooper the finest house he could have builded." Since it was a common assumption among "philanthropists, Professors, and Lady Millionaires" in this era that there was just so much money around and the real problem of the day was its division, it would be more deserving to devote the funds spent for the large house to the production of decencies for the people rather than "to pad the couch, and pamper the appetite of indolence." Defenders of luxurious expenditures thought the actuality of the situation quite different. If the labor called forth in providing the big house and its appurtenances were devoted to the production of necessities, there would be too much of the latter and the country "'would be smothered in its own grease'; all might fatten alike upon the gross product of mere animal necessities, without mental development or progress of any kind." Furthermore the implication that the presence of the big house meant the existence of the hovel was unsound. As a Professor of Economics at Boston University snapped, "The notion there is necessarily any causal connection between opulence and poverty is too crude to require serious refutation."

However sharp the reproof, the critics of the big house still thought it an evil to be crushed. They were given pause by the realization that the capitalist's bad motives, of selfishness and vanity, nonetheless spurred his productive faculties. "As long as the vanity of wealth is a ruling motive for its acquisition," concluded John Bascom, president of the University of Wisconsin, "we cannot expect nor do

the interests of production suffer us to wish that luxury should be restrained, or any more generous impulses be forced on industry, than those of the social state which sustain it. Our remedy is not physical but moral; not in economic regulations, but in enlarged culture." Henry George joined in the aversion to any "sumptuary legislation" on the matter of housing.

Others of a bolder and less thoughtful temper flirted with the idea that at least a ceiling should be placed on the amount a millionaire could spend for a house. However much such direct intervention challenged deep American folkways, there was a strain in American thought which justified it. Prohibition of expenditures for alcohol was often motivated by the concern of the employer with the habits and expenses of his employee and by the concern of the big taxpayer with the expensive maintenance of the chronically inebriated. But was it not true also that the rich drank as much champagne as the poor did lager beer? Into the clamor of such *tu quoque*'s Atkinson moved with the serenity of his ubiquitous calculations. No matter what he receives in income,

a man costs only what he consumes. . . . The question may well be asked, What class wastes the most, the rich in their luxurious personal expenditure, or the mass of the people who spend a sum variously computed at $700,000,-000 to $1,000,000,000 a year on spirits, beer and tobacco? So far as any computation is possible, in my judgment, the annual product, *i.e.,* the wage and profit fund, is impaired more seriously by the waste of the poor and ignorant, . . . than by all the luxurious expenditure of the rich.

In view of the complexities in preventing a man from spending his money as he pleased, it was more feasible to prevent him from having so much money to spend. Here taxation was the key. The statement of Justice Stephen J. Field in the income tax decision of 1895 that such a tax was "an assault upon capital" has occasioned much derision, then and since. In view of the percentage level of the tax, 2 per cent upon incomes over $4,000, Field's assertion was surely so much an overstatement as to be ludicrous. In all likelihood the many motives which lay behind the statute contained those elements of envy and disapproval of the use of wealth which the issue of the big house had raised. "Let those pay the taxes who reap out of the nation more than they need," a laboring man had declared in the previous decade, and a manufacturer would tax the millionaires so heavily that extravagant living would be impossible. "I maintain that a person can go through this life with an income of $25,000 per annum very comfortably."

Clearly such responses came naturally to those whose income was used up in day-by-day expenditures on consumption. They revealed, however, a complete ignorance of the economic order and how it worked. The income of rich men was not usually dissipated in riotous and extravagant living; it was employed in trade and industry. As Charles Elliott Perkins wrote in 1891, the money Huntington and Gould accumulated "does them personally very little good—a small part of their incomes may be wasted in show or champagne, but most of it is invested in some form of industry which directly benefits the masses by making something cheaper." "Natural law" insures that the tendency of wealth is to reproduce itself. According to this school of thought the criticism of the expenditures of rich men, of which the big house was a symbol, was an irrelevance, except for the censorious, the envious, and the merely worried. Within the business community, nonetheless, there was occasional uneasiness at the current architectural exhibitionism. Carnegie, with the cosmic air he customarily gave to his utterances, held forth upon the historical disadvantages of "long-continued prosperity," the chief of which was "the reign of luxury and the vices it breeds." Great Britain had already entered that phase. With civilization had come "the contrast between the palace and the cottage of the laborer." Since this was the necessary price for progress, it is "the duty of the man of Wealth: First to set an example of modest, unostentatious living, shunning display or extravagance." It is true "the star-spangled Scotchman" had no yacht, no opera box, no old masters and first editions. But he did have a home with a garden and lawn on upper Fifth Avenue, and a castle in Scotland on an estate of 32,000 acres. Like Atkinson, Carnegie knew that millionaires must cost something.

HENRY DAVID (b. 1907) is a renowned educator and labor specialist. He began his career at Columbia University, and later became dean of the Graduate Faculty at the New School for Social Research and then its president. He now serves as executive secretary of the Division of Behavioral Sciences of the National Academy of Science and as a consultant to the Rand Corporation. His extensive writings on labor include *Labor Problems in America* (1940), *House of Labor* (1951), and *Manpower Politics for a Democratic Society* (1965). In this selection, taken from his first book, he attributes the worker's problems to a growing impersonalization created by the rise of big business and the pursuit of wealth.*

Henry David

The Tyrant Cracks the Whip

The changes in industrial technique led to the increase of factory laborers, who in contrast to the handicraft worker, may be regarded as semi-skilled or un-skilled. Differentiation between employer and employee became more striking, and the dominant conception of the worker as an impersonal commodity became more sharply confirmed. In M. A. Foran's *The Other Side, A Social Study Based on Fact,* published in 1886, a note-worthy though poorly conceived labor novel which is strongly pro-working class, but not opposed to capitalism as such, social cleavage between employers and employees is a constant theme. Antagonistic to radical doctrines, the novel

nevertheless presents the average employer of the period just as unfavorably as did the revolutionary of the day, describing him as a domineering "master."

The gulf which separated workingman and employer, either individual or corporate, was produced by the economic changes which the country had experienced. In some occupations it was a comparatively recent development. A brassworker discussing this question in 1883, remarked: "Well, I remember that fourteen years ago the workmen and foremen and the boss were all as one happy family; it was just as easy and as free to speak to the boss as anyone else, but now the boss is superior, and the men

*From Henry David, *The History of the Haymarket Affair: A Study in the American Social-Revolutionary and Labor Movements* [1936]. Second edition, New York: Russell and Russell, 1958, pp. 6–12, 20–24. Footnotes omitted.

all go to the foremen; but we would not think of looking the foreman in the face now any more than we would the boss. . . . The average hand growing up in the shop now would not think of speaking to the boss, would not presume to recognize him, nor the boss would not recognize him either." Employers "adopt a superior stand-point," complained another workingman. "The employer has pretty much the same feeling towards the men that he had toward his machinery. He wants to get as much as he can out of his men at the cheapest rate. . . . That is all he cares for the man generally."

One manufacturer bluntly declared, according to Samuel Gompers, "I regard my employes as I do a machine, to be used to my advantage, and when they are old and of no further use I cast them in the street." The indifference to human values here displayed was neither an invention of Gompers nor wholly exceptional. A New England wool-manufacturer, complacently observed that when workers "get starved down to it, then they will go to work at just what you can afford to pay." Such views accompanied the conviction that it is, as Jay Gould said, an "axiom . . . that labor is a commodity that will in the long run be governed absolutely by the law of supply and demand," —an argument which justified adequately the manner in which workers were commonly treated. Labor was a commodity—though sometimes a peculiar and troublesome one—and there was no reason why it should be dealt with differently from other commodities. ". . . I never do my talking to the hands," said a New England mill owner, "I do all my talking with the overseers."

As long as these attitudes were taken by a considerable body of employers, it is no wonder that the feeling between them and the workers was generally one of steadily increasing "distrust and dissatisfaction," as Joseph Medill, publisher of the Chicago *Tribune*, put it. P. J. Mc Guire, a labor leader, was no less aware of the absence of amicable relations between workers and employers. Their respective activities and wealth—or lack of it—drove a powerful wedge between them. They had no social contacts. "They do not know each other on the street." The more poorly paid workers, observed W. H. Foster, general secretary of the Federation of Organized Trades and Labor Unions, in 1883, exhibited an attitude of "sullen discontent" toward those who employed them. "They do not seem to have the courage to express openly what they think all the time, unless they are under the influence of liquor."

In pre-Civil War days industry was smaller in scope; less of it was corporately organized; the independent artisan was still an important industrial factor; and escape from working-class ranks was less difficult. The relationship of employer and employee of that period had almost vanished by the 'eighties. As one writer sympathetic to labor observed of the 'eighties and 'nineties, "the old liberality of American employers is on the wane. Competition compels them to be closefisted and to inaugurate a policy of aggressive resistance against the demands of organized labor." As labor, becoming increasingly conscious of its condition, boldly voiced its complaints and demands, and resorted more widely to industrial action to gain its objectives, capital developed not only the normal defense mechanisms but a definite militancy. In an age dedicated to the business exploitation of the vast resources of America it would have been strange had there not been an aggressive capitalist class. The spirit of the Gilded Age can be understood when it is remembered that the business men of the period were pioneers —pioneers in industry, pioneers in the pursuit of wealth.

The idealization of property so characteristic of the period was a natural result of the intensive pursuit of material possessions. Walt Whitman declared that "Democracy looks with suspicious, ill-satisfied eyes upon the very poor and on those out of business; she asks for men and women with occupations, well off, owners of houses and acres, and with cash in the bank." John Hay's *The Bread-Winners,* with its hostile treatment of discontented labor, its "odor of property-morality," was a natural and early literary manifestation of this attitude. Josiah Strong remarked that the "Christian man who is not willing to make the largest profits which an honest regard for the laws of trade permits is a rare man." To the charge that the Vanderbilts' wealth was a monstrous injustice in a democratic republic, one writer replied that "Mr. Vanderbilt is receiving a proportionally small, and a well earned part of the profits of the greatest economical device of modern times." He was merely being rewarded for his father's great services to mankind and more particularly to American society.

That tremendous appetite for wealth, which showed its worst side in the operations of Jay Gould, was amusingly satirized in the following bit of doggerel:

JAY GOULD'S MODEST WANTS

My wants are few; I scorn to be
    A querulous refiner;
I only want America
    And a mortgage deed of China;
And if kind fate threw Europe in,
    And Africa and Asia,
And a few islands of the sea,
    I'd ask no other treasure.
Give me but these—they are enough
    To suit my notion—

And I'll give up to other men
    All land beneath the ocean.

The arrogance of wealth is illustrated by the words attributed to an American millionaire of the 'eighties who said of his class: "We are not politicians or public thinkers; we are the rich; we own America; we got it, God knows how, but we intend to keep it if we can. . . ." The cry that American labor shared inadequately in the industrial wealth of the nation and that a large portion of the laboring class was impoverished was either never heard or flatly denied by capital. Andrew Carnegie, addressing the Nineteenth Century Club at the close of 1887, exclaimed, "I defy any man to show that there is pauperism" in the United States. William Graham Sumner, closing his eyes to incontrovertible evidence, declared that pauperism did not characterize the American wage-earning class. "It is constantly alleged in vague and declamatory terms," he wrote, "that artisans and unskilled laborers are in distress and misery, or are under oppression. No facts to bear out these assertions are offered."

If they admitted the existence of poverty among a considerable portion of the working-class, business men were ready to ascribe it to inadequate education, drink, laziness, and improvidence. Occasionally, they placed part of the responsibility upon the activities of manipulators and gamblers who were not to be confused with sober, honest industrialists. Joseph Medill declared that the primary "cause of the impecunious condition of millions of wage classes of this country is due to their own improvidence and misdirected efforts. Too many are trying to live without labor . . . and too many squander their earnings on intoxicating drinks, cigars and amusements, who cannot afford it." It was easy to place the responsibility for inadequate wages and penury upon unalterable economic laws which determined the share that labor received. Thus, the Commercial Club of Boston was informed that

There is certainly a very general complaint just now that labor does not get its share, that capital gets more than its share, that things ought not to go on as they have gone. . . . But complaints are not always well founded. Men as well as children often desire what they cannot and ought not to have. And complaining settles nothing. The existing mode of division is the work of certain natural laws. . . .

It is perfectly right for the wage earner to get all he can. The employer will pay as little as he can. . . . It is the duty of the employer to sedulously regard the interests of those he employs, to deal fairly by them. Above all, every man imbued with the spirit of Christianity, the Christian in deed as well as in name, will strive to do as he would be done by.

But after all, one inexorable law finally settles this as it does so many other economic questions, and that is the law of demand and supply.

Not everyone, however, denied that the American worker had just ground for complaint, or ascribed such unfortunate conditions as existed to the operation of natural laws. In his first annual report in 1886, Commissioner Wright, discussing the effect of the industrial revolution upon the worker, declared that "if the question should be asked, has the wageworker received his equitable share of the benefits derived from the introduction of machinery, the answer must be no. In the struggle for industrial supremacy in the great countries devoted to mechanical production, it probably has been impossible for him to share equitably in such benefits." Some of the State bureaus of labor or labor statistics pointed to evidences of the maldistribution of wealth, and concluded that labor did not receive a fair share in the returns of industry. Such assertions were made by the bureau of New Jersey in 1881 and 1883, of Illinois in 1882, and of Michigan in 1884. Some writers charged that State and Federal laws favored the few at the expense of the many. In an article in the *Contemporary Review,* Prof. Charles Kendall Adams reported that in 1886 a "very large proportion of our thoughtful writers were inclined to take it for granted that the wageworkers had a grievance that could, in some way, be corrected. The opinion was very general that . . . the masses of the people did not receive their fair share . . ." When Francis A. Walker asserted that the "real labor problem of today" turned on the question of how the self-assertiveness of the working-class could be tempered, he made it clear that it was "rightful," and that it would make for an "equitable and beneficial distribution of wealth" which was then lacking.

Labor's grievances sprang from the privileges and corruption of the American political system, the growth of a small, immensely wealthy class, the results of corporate industrial organization, and the economic and social condition of the wage-earners at large and certain groups of them in particular. Protests against monopolies and large corporations filled the air during the period. The latter were denounced as sources of "outrage" and "corruption" and destroyers of human rights. National and State governments, it was charged, had been captured by corporate interests, for whose benefit they legislated at the expense of the many. The courts were stigmatized as subservient tools of the vested interests. A contributor to the *Catholic Quar-*

terly Review summed up current attitudes in the assertion that "it is futile for the public press to be constantly preaching platitudes respecting patience and regard for the rights of the employers and respect for the law, whilst evasions and defiant violations, constantly practised by mammoth capitalists and corporations, are ignored, condoned and tacitly approved." . . .

Most industrial problems and most labor discontent arose in connection with the primary questions of employment, wages and hours. There were, however, other sources of antagonism between employer and worker in the secondary conditions of labor and in a number of industrial practises to which employers resorted. The latter include the black-list, the iron-clad oath and the practise of assessing fines and charges. While these affected only some workers, they called forth protests from American labor at large.

Fining, most common in retail stores, hotels, and restaurants, was also found in factories, generally only in those employing large numbers of women and children. Workers were fined for coming late, for being absent without permission, for singing or talking with one another during working hours, for unusual noise, for imperfections in the work, and for a host of arbitrary reasons. Fines were sometimes assessed to the extent of two and three per cent of the weekly wages, without any statement of the reasons for their imposition. It is true, of course, that fining affected industry to a minor extent at this time, and there was almost none of it among male factory workers. It was most in evidence in the older manufacturing States, but was spreading to all. In severely condemning the system in 1886, the Bureau of Labor Statistics of Illinois pointed out that fining was a development of the past five years, and that while it had not yet made deep inroads, the practise was growing rapidly.

A series of investigations by the Chicago *Times* of the factories of Chicago, especially those employing women and children, disclosed in 1888 that the fining practise had spread. Frequently employees lost a considerable portion of the $3–4 weekly they received for a ten hour day through fines.

Other burdensome charges were levied upon employees. Female operatives, especially in the clothing industry, were sometimes forced to contribute a certain per cent of the weekly wage to pay for the machines upon which they worked. If the worker left her employ before the machine was paid for, she usually forfeited her "contributions." Payments for needles and thread were common, and frequently workers were required to cover the expense of repairing machines. In at least one instance, the employer levied a charge of twenty-five cents weekly upon each operative for the steam by which the factory was run. There were authenticated instances where female operatives lost one-half of their weekly wages—which generally came to about five dollars—because of such charges. Another practise, also found widely among female workers, compelled new hands to turn over a portion of the first week's wages as surety against quitting the factory before the expiration of a six months' period or without giving two weeks' notice. If the proper notice were given or six months had elapsed, the money was returned. Where this rule was rigidly enforced, an employee would lose the sum deposited for failing to report to work on any one day before the half year was up.

The iron-clad oath, comparable to the yellow-dog contract of the present day, was employed to prevent the unionization of factories and shops. The oath affirmed that the signer was not a member of a labor organization, did not contemplate joining and would never join one. In its broadest sense it prohibited the members of a shop from collective action or even consultation of any kind. It was usually accompanied by a pernicious system of spying by which employers were informed of infractions of the oath. Membership in a labor organization of any sort was, for one who had signed it, cause for instant dismissal. Where labor organizations were weak or were in process of formation, the iron-clad oath was a particularly potent weapon. Workers had no legal redress against it. It was successfully used on many occasions to drive workers out of their organizations, or at least make such membership secret.

Against the black-list the worker was given statutory protection by some States and in practically all of them its use could be prosecuted as a conspiracy punishable at common law. Few wage-earners were cognizant of this, however, and court action was rarely taken. In essence, the black-list was the employers' method of boycotting obnoxious workers. Names on the list were circularized among employers within the same trade, and workers thus distinguished found it impossible to secure employment within a given district or even in other regions. Commonly regarded by workers as the cause of the labor boycott, to which it was analogous, the black-list was employed almost solely against men engaged in union activities. It served, therefore, as a supplementary weapon to the iron-clad oath. In the 'eighties, and especially by 1886, it was increasingly popular among employers. It was most bitterly resented in organized labor circles, which regarded its employment as a blanket declaration of war against union labor by the employer. Employers also often imported foreign and colored workers into a troublesome locality to prevent the formation of labor organizations or destroy those which already existed.

A limited number of workers found a grievance in the fact that they received their wages partly in cash and partly in goods or orders for goods. This practise obtained largely in the coal industry, where the company store system was frequently found with it. In Illinois, about one-fifth of the wage-earners in the coal industry were subject to the burdens of the system. In most instances, these stores sold goods at prices above those prevailing in the locality, and frequently they profiteered to the extent of twenty per cent above normal prices. In many regions, reported Carroll D. Wright in 1886, "employment depends partially upon taking goods out of the companies' stores." Large numbers of workers likewise found the custom of paying wages at fortnightly or monthly intervals burdensome, and some States passed laws to protect the worker from employers who withheld his earnings for too long a time.

Obviously, not all American workers were being subjected to the unjust conditions which produced the working-class discontent of the period. But the unpleasant elements in the industrial scene cannot be glossed over, and the latter cannot be presented in the roseate light in which many of its contemporaries saw it. The American worker, it is true, was less rigidly fixed in his economic class and function than the European; passage into another class was easier for him; he enjoyed a degree of social equality and freedom, as well as material advantages, which the European did not. All this was frequently pointed out at the time. Yet it does not follow that the American workingman had no reason for complaint, or that he was not conscious of the inequalities in American society. In 1888, James Bryce observed that

There are no struggles between privileged and unprivileged orders, not even that perpetual strife of rich and poor. . . . No one of the questions which now agitate the nation is a question between rich and poor. Instead of suspicion, jealousy, and arrogance embittering the relations of classes, good feeling and kindliness reign. Everything that government, as the Americans have . . . understood the term, can give them, the poorer class have already. . . . Hence the poorer have had little to fight for, no grounds for disliking the well-to-do, few complaints to make against them.

Bryce placed upon the shoulders of foreigners who brought "their Old World passions with them," responsibility for the cries of protest which were raised and the labor disturbances which occurred.

His judgments, however, cannot be accepted as either adequate or accurate. The elements which disturbed the serenity of the industrial scene were not exceptional to it—they cannot be regarded as rare abnormalities—and it was not alone the "foreigner" who was cognizant of them. If the worker aired his grievances, it was because he had full reason. America had reached a stage in economic development where a tranquil industrial life and a contented working class were practical impossibilities.

HERBERT GUTMAN (b. 1928), Professor of history at the University of Rochester, is an authority on the relationship between industrialization and social change in the United States between 1869 and 1890. In a series of articles, he has questioned the traditional labor picture of the Gilded Ages as portrayed by David. He sees the reality as more complex, with public attitudes toward labor shaped to a large extent by the social setting. An impersonal and consequently harsh labor relationship was established more easily in urban than in rural areas, which experienced a "value lag" in adopting the new social order. How effectively does Gutman modify David's judgment on labor conditions?*

Herbert Gutman

A Reconsideration of Labor Policies

A rather stereotyped conception of labor and of industrial relations in the Gilded Age has gained widespread credence. Final and conclusive generalizations about labor abound. A labor economist describes industrial conflict in the 1870's in an authoritative fashion:

During the depression from 1873 to 1879, employers sought to eliminate trade unions by a *systematic* policy of lock outs, blacklists, labor espionage, and legal prosecution. The *widespread* use of blacklists and Pinkerton labor spies caused labor to organize *more or less* secretly, and *undoubtedly* helped bring on the violence that *characterized* labor strife during this period. [Emphasis added.]

A labor historian asserts, "Employers *everywhere* seemed determined to rid themselves of 'restrictions upon free enterprise' by smashing unions." The "*typical* [labor] organization during the seventies," writes another scholar, "was secret for protection against intrusion by outsiders." Such seemingly final judgments are very questionable. How *systematic* were lockouts, blacklists, and legal prosecutions? How *widespread* was the use of labor spies and private detectives? Was the secret union the *typical* form of labor organization? Did violence *characterize* industrial relations?

It is widely believed that the industrialist exercised a great deal of power and had almost unlimited freedom of choice when dealing with his workers

*Selections reprinted by permission of the publisher from "The Worker's Search for Power: Labor in the Gilded Age," by Herbert Gutman in *The Gilded Age,* edited by H. Wayne Morgan (Syracuse, N.Y.: Syracuse University Press, 1963), pp. 39–48, 67–68. Footnotes omitted.

after the Civil War. Part of this belief reflects the weakness or absence of trade unions. Another justification for this interpretation, however, is somewhat more shaky. It is the assumption that industrialism generated new kinds of economic power which, in turn, *immediately* affected the social structure and the ideology of that time. The supposition that "interests" rapidly reshaped "ideas" is entirely too simple and therefore misleading. "The social pyramid," Joseph Schumpeter pointed out, "is never made of a single substance, is never seamless." There is no single *Zeitgeist*, except in the sense of a construct. The economic interpretation of history "would at once become untenable and unrealistic . . . if its formulation failed to consider that the manner in which production shapes social life is essentially influenced by the fact that human protagonists have always been shaped by past situations." Too often, the study of industrial development and industrial relations in the Gilded Age has neglected these pertinent strictures.

Careful study of a number of small industrial communities in this era suggests that the relationships between "interest" and "ideology" was very complex and subtle. In this period, industrial capitalism was relatively new as a total way of life and therefore was not fully institutionalized. Much of the history of industrialism at that time is the story of the painful process by which an old way of life was discarded for a new one. The central issue was the rejection or modification of an old set of "rules" and "commands" which no longer fit the new industrial context. Since so much was new, traditional stereotypes about the popular sanctioning of the rules and values of industrial society either demand severe qualification or entirely fall by the wayside. Among questionable commonly held generalizations are those that insist that the worker was isolated from the rest of society; that the employer had an easy time and a relatively free hand in imposing the new disciplines; that the spirit of the times, the ethic of the Gilded Age, worked to the advantage of the owner of industrial property; that workers found little if any sympathy from nonworkers; that the quest for wealth obliterated nonpecuniary values; and that industrialists swept aside countless obstacles with great ease. The usual picture of these years portrays the absolute power of the employer over his workers and emphasizes his ability to manipulate a sympathetic public opinion as well as various political, legal, and social institutions to his advantage.

The story is not so simple, however, as intensive examination of numerous strikes and lockouts shows. The new way of life was more popular and more quickly sanctioned in large cities than in small towns dominated by one or two industries. Put another way, the social environment in the large American city after the Civil War was more often hostile toward workers than was that in the smaller industrial towns. Employers in large cities had more freedom of choice than their counterparts in small towns where local conditions of one kind or another often hampered the employer's decision-making power. The ideology of many nonworkers in these small towns was not entirely hospitable toward industrial, as opposed to traditional, business enterprise. Strikes and lockouts in large cities seldom lasted as long as similar disputes outside of these urban centers. In the large city, there was almost no sympathy for the city worker from the middle and upper classes. At the same time, a good deal of pro-labor and anti-industrial sentiment (the two are not necessarily the same) flowed from similar occupational groups in the small towns. It is a commonplace that the small-town employer of factory labor often reached out of his local environment for aid of one kind or another in solving industrial disputes, but insufficient attention has been given to these elements in the contemporary social structure and ideology which shaped such decisions.

Though the direct economic relationships in large cities and in small towns and outlying industrial regions were essentially similar, the social structure in each of these areas was profoundly different. Here is the crucial clue to these distinct patterns of thought and behavior. Private enterprise was central to the economy of the small industrial town as well as to that of the large metropolitan city, but it functioned in a different social environment. The social structure and ideology of a given time are not derived only from economic institutions. In the Gilded Age, a time of rapid economic and social transformation and a time when industrial capitalism was still young and relatively new to the United States, parts of an ideology that were alien to the new industrialism retained a powerful hold on the minds of many who lived outside the large cities. . . .

More than economic considerations shaped the status of the working population in large cities after the Civil War, for the social structure there unavoidably widened the distance between the various social and economic classes. Home and job often were far apart. A man's fellow workers often differed from his friends and neighbors. Face-to-face relationships became less meaningful as the city grew larger and as production became more diverse and more specialized. "It has always been difficult for well-to-do peo-ple of the upper and middle classes," wrote Samuel Lane Loomis, a Protestant minister, in the 1880's, "to sympathize and to understand the needs of their poorer neighbors." The large city, both impersonal and confining, made it even harder. Loomis was convinced that "a great and growing gulf" lay "between the working-class and those above them." A Massachusetts clergyman saw a similar void between the social classes and complained: "I once knew a wealthy manufacturer who personally visited and looked after the comforts of his invalid operatives. I know of no such case now." All in all, the fabric of human relationships was cloaked in a kind of shadowed anonymity that became more and more characteristic of urban life.

Social contact was more direct in the smaller post-Civil War industrial towns and regions. The *Cooper's New Monthly,* a reform trade-union journal, insisted that while "money" was the "sole measure of gentility and respectability" in large cities "a more democratic feeling" prevailed in small towns. "The most happy and contented workingmen in the country," wrote the *Iron Molder's Journal,* "are those residing in small towns and villages. . . . We want more towns and less cities." Except for certain parts of New England the mid-Atlantic states, the post-Civil War industrial towns and regions were relatively new to that kind of enterprise. The men and women who lived and worked in these areas in the Gilded Age usually had known another way of life and doggedly contrasted the present with the past. They grasped the realities of the new industrialism for a simple reason: the nineteenth-century notion of enterprise came quickly to these regions after the Civil War, but the social distance between the various economic classes that characterized the large city came much more slowly and hardly paralleled industrial developments. In the midst of the new industrial enterprise with its new set of commands, therefore, men often clung to an older ("agrarian") set of values. They often judged the economic and social behavior of local industrialists by these older and more humane values. The social structure of the large city differed from that of the small industrial town because of the more direct human relationships among the residents of the smaller towns. Although many of these persons were not personally involved in the industrial process, they always felt its presence. Life may have been more difficult and less cosmopolitan in these small towns, but it was also less complicated. This life was not romantic, for it frequently meant company-owned houses and stores as well as conflicts between workers and employers over rights that were taken for granted in agricultural communities and large cities. Yet, the nonurban industrial environment had in it a kind of compelling simplicity. Its inhabitants lived and worked together, and a certain sense of community threaded their everyday lives. Men knew each other well, and the anonymity that veiled so much of urban life was not nearly so severe. There was of course more than enough economic hardship and plain despair in these towns, but the impersonal social environment of the large city in the Gilded Age was almost entirely lacking. . . .

In cutting costs in 1873 and 1874, many employers faced difficult problems, but a central trouble emerged when they found that certain aspects of the social structure and ideology in small industrial towns hindered their freedom of action. It proved relatively easy for them to announce a wage cut or to refuse publicly to negotiate with a local trade union, but it often proved quite difficult to enforce such decisions easily and quickly. In instance after instance, and for reasons that varied from region to region, employers reached outside of their local environment to help assert their local authority.

Industrialists used various methods to strengthen their local positions with their workers. The state militia brought order to a town or region swept by industrial conflict. Troops were used in railroad strikes in Indiana, Ohio, and Pennsylvania; in a dispute involving iron heaters and rollers in Newport, Kentucky; in a strike of Colorado ore diggers; in two strikes of Illinois coal miners; and in a strike of Michigan ore workers. At the same time, other employers aggravated racial and nationality problems among workers by introducing new ethnic groups in their towns as a way of ending strikes, forcing men to work under new contracts, and destroying local trade unions. Negroes were used in coal disputes. Danish, Norwegian, and Swedish immigrants were brought into mines in Illinois, and into the Shenango Valley and the northern anthracite region of Pennsylvania. Germans went to coal mines in northern Ohio along with Italian workers. Some Italians also were used in western and northern New York as railroad workers. A number of employers imposed their authority in other ways. Regional not local blacklists were tried in the Illinois coal fields, on certain railroads, in the Ohio Valley iron towns, and in the iron mills of eastern Pennsylvania. Mine operators in Pennsylvania's Shenango Valley and Tioga coal region used state laws that allowed them to evict discontented workers from company-owned houses in mid-winter.

In good part, the social structure in these small towns and the ideology of many of their residents, who were neither workers nor employeers, shaped the behavior of those employers who reached outside their local environments in order to win industrial disputes. The story is different for every town, but has certain similarities. The strikes and lockouts had little meaning in and of themselves, and it is of passing interest to learn whether the employers or the workers gained a victory. The incidents assume broader significance as they shed light on the distribution of power in these towns and on those important social and economic relationships which shaped the attitudes and actions of workers and employers.

One neglected aspect of the small industrial town after the Civil War is its political structure. Because workers made up a large proportion of the electorate and often participated actively in local politics, they were able at times to influence local and regional affairs in a manner not open to wage-earners in the larger cities. There is no evidence in 1874 that workers held elected or appointed offices in large cities. In that year, nevertheless, the postmaster of Whistler, Alabama, was a member of the Iron Molder's International Union. George Kinghorn, a leading trade-unionist in the southern Illinois coal fields, was postmaster of West Belleville, Illinois. A local labor party swept an election in Evansville, Indiana. Joliet, Illinois, had three workers on its city council. A prominent official of the local union of iron heaters and rollers sat on the city council in Newport, Kentucky. Coal and ore miners ran for the state legislature in Carthage, Missouri, in Clay County, Indiana, and in Belleville, Illinois. The residents of Virginia City, a town famous to western mythology, sent the president of the local union of miners to the national Congress. In other instances, town officials and other office-holders who were not wage-earners sympathized with the problems and difficulties of local workers or displayed an unusual degree of objectivity during local industrial disputes.

It was the same with many local newspapers in these towns, for they often stood apart from the industrial entrepreneur and subjected his behavior to searching criticisms. Editorials in these journals defended *local* workers and demanded redress for their grievances. Certain of these newspapers were entirely independent in their outlook, and others warmly endorsed local trade-union activities.

The small businessmen and shopkeepers, the lawyers and professional people, and the other nonindustrial members of the middle class were a small but vital element in these industrial towns. Unlike the urban middle class they had direct and everyday contact with the new industrialism and with the problems and the outlook of workers and employers. Many had risen from a lower station in life and intimately knew the meaning of hardship and toil. They could judge the troubles and complaints of both workers and employers by personal experience and by what happened around them and did not have to rely on secondary accounts. While they invariably accepted the concepts of private property and free entrepreneurship, their judgments about the *social* behavior of industrialists often drew upon noneconomic considerations and values. They saw no necessary contradiction between private enterprise and gain on the one hand, and decent, humane social relations between workers and employers on the other. In a number of industrial conflicts, segments of the local middle class sided with the workers in their communities. A Maryland weekly newspaper complained in 1876, "In the changes of the last thirty years not the least unfortunate is the separation of personal relations between employers and employees." At the same time that most metropolitan newspapers sang paeans of joy for the industrial entrepreneur and the new way of life, the *Youngstown Miner and Manufacturer* thought it completely wrong that the "Vanderbilts, Stewarts, and Astors bear, in proportion to their resources, infinitely less of the burden incident to society than the poorest worker." The *Ironton Register* defended dismissed iron strikers as "upright and esteemed . . . citizens" who had been sacrificed "to the cold demands on business." The *Portsmouth Times* boasted, "We have very little of the codfish aristocracy, and industrious laborers are looked upon here with as much respect as any class of people." . . .

There is much to say about the attitude toward labor that existed in large cities, but over all opinion lay a popular belief that iron laws governed not only the economy but life itself, and that he who tampered with them through social experiments or reforms imperiled the whole structure. The *Chicago Times* was honest if perhaps callous in saying: "Whatever cheapens production, whatever will lessen the cost of growing wheat, digging gold, washing dishes, building steam engines, is of value. . . . The age is not one which enquires when looking at a piece of lace whether the woman who wove it is a saint or a courtesan." It came at last almost to a kind of inhumanity, as one manufacturer who used dogs as well as men in his operation discovered. The employer liked the dogs better than the men. "They never go on strike for higher wages, have no labor unions, never get intoxicated and disorderly, never absent themselves from work without good cause, obey orders without growling, and are very reliable."

The contrast between urban and rural views of labor and its fullest role in society and life is clear. In recent years, many have stressed "entrepreneurship" in nineteenth-century America without distinguishing between entrepreneurs in commerce and trade and entrepreneurs in industrial manufacturing. Reflecting the stresses and strains in the thought and social attitudes of a generation passing from the old agricultural way of life to the new industrial America, many men could justify the business ethic in its own sphere without sustaining it in operation in society at large or in human relationships. It was one thing to apply brute force in the market place, and quite another to talk blithely of "iron laws" in operation when men's lives and well-being were at stake.

Not all men had such second thoughts about the social fabric which industrialism and commercialism were weaving, but in the older areas of the country, still susceptible to the cries of an ancient conscience, the spirits of free enterprise and free action were neither dead nor mutually exclusive. As the story shows clearly, many elements of labor kept their freedom of action and bargaining even during strikes. And the worker was not without shrewdness in his appeal to public opinion. There is a certain irony in realizing that rural, or at least small-town America, supposedly alien and antagonistic toward the city and its ways, remained in this period a stronghold of freedom for the worker seeking his economic and social rights.

But perhaps this is not so strange after all, for rural America, whatever its narrowness and faults, had always preached individualism and personal freedom. It was the city, whose very impersonality would one day make it a kind of frontier of anonymity, which often preached personal restriction and the law of the economic and social jungle. As industrialism triumphed, the businessman's powers increased, yet it is significant that in this generation of genuine freedom of action, he was often hindered and always suspect in vast areas of the nation which cheered his efforts toward wealth even while often frustating his methods.

Facile generalizations are easy to make and not always sound, but surely the evidence warrants a new view of labor in the Gilded Age. The standard stereotypes and textbook cliches about its impotence and division before the iron hand of oppressive capitalism do not fit the facts. Its story is far different when surveyed in depth, carrying in it overtones of great complexity. And it is not without haunting and instructive reminders that even in an age often dominated by lusts for power, men did not forget or abandon old and honored concepts of human dignity and worth.

GUSTAVUS MYERS (1872–1942), during the investigation for *The History of Tammany Hall* (1917), decided to broaden his inquiry into the methods used in amassing great fortunes from the colonial period to his day. While Myers claimed that he wanted only political reform, he leaned in a Marxist direction. After completing his *History of the Great American Fortunes,* he searched long and hard for a publisher willing to run the risk of possible attack. Finally, in 1910, Charles H. Kerr released the work in three volumes. Myers actually viewed the United States in an optimistic light. In his *History of American Idealism* (1925) he traced the historical abolition of inequality and made a plea for economic equality. After reading this selection from *History of the Great American Fortunes,* do you agree with Myers that much of the wealth garnered by Collis Huntington, Leland Stanford, Mark Hopkins, and Charles Crocker resulted from bribery and intimidation of politicians.*

Gustavus Myers

The Moguls Manipulate Congress

[Collis Huntington, Leland Stanford, Mark Hopkins, and Charles Crocker] had migrated from the East to California after the discovery of gold on the Pacific Coast. There Huntington carried on a hardware and miners' supply store at Sacramento, and Hopkins became his partner; Crocker was likewise a small merchant, and Stanford was a lawyer. The four were not able to scrape together a pool of more than an insignificant sum with which to execute what was then considered one of the greatest and most difficult railroad projects of modern times.

The phrase monger is addicted to rhapsodizing upon the marvelous self-confidence which could initiate a huge railroad line with only a trivial sum as a starter. This may be a romantic way of describing their prowess and ingenuity. But neither was the project itself of their conception, nor did they have to supply the funds. Years before they took hold of the work as a definite undertaking, the building of Pacific lines had been agitated and urged, and the Government had surveyed feasible routes. Not one of the quartet knew anything of railroad construction, nor had the least fundamental knowledge of how to equip and operate a railroad.

In what direction, then, lay their ability? Purely and wholly in the line of promoting. The capitalist system was of such a fantastically inverted nature that to

*From *History of the Great American Fortunes,* by Gustavus Myers. Copyright 1909, 1910 and renewed 1936, 1937 by Gustavus Myers. Reprinted by permission of Random House, Inc., pp. 126–137. Footnotes omitted.

grasp the ownership of anything did not imply or require the ability of supervision. Railroads, factories, mines and public utility systems were generally owned by men—often by absentees—who knew nothing of any aspect of them except the one all-important phase—the budget of profit or loss.

The ability of the promoter was the most necessary consideration, although not the foremost in insuring the title of ownership. Very frequently, in the case of factories and mines, promoters had to get funds from banking houses, which usually, by skillful law work, succeeded in getting those promoters into a legal snare, forcing them out, and expropriating their property. Railroad promoters, however, did not have to depend so much upon private bankers. They could draw upon Government, State and cities for advances of money. If a man, or a set of men, could succeed in bribing Congress and the legislatures to donate land grants and advance the funds, it was a very simple matter to hire highly competent civil engineers to survey and build the routes, and employ good executives to run them after they were built.

The first and prime necessity was the purchase of legislation with its corollaries—franchises, gifts and free access to the public treasuries. This done, the remainder of the program was easy. In this regard it was that Huntington and his partners showed their finesse—not an unusual finesse, by any means, its caliber was neither more nor less than that of many another capitalist, who also had been adroit in bribing legislation through.

Upon organizing the Central Pacific Railroad Company in 1861, the Huntington group could not privately raise more than about $195,000, of which amount they, themselves, put in about

$50,000. This sum, ridiculously inadequate to build a railraod estimated to cost $25,000,000, was, however, enough and more than enough, for certain well-understood primary operations.

With it expenses could be defrayed at the centers of legislation; petitions and memorials concocted; advocates paid, and newspapers subsidized. If the trick were well turned, a whole succession of franchises, special laws, land grants and money subsidies would follow. Thus we see that the original capital needed in many capitalist enterprises was not for the actual prosecution of the work, but for the purpose of bribery. In fact, money, as an absolute requirement, could be dispensed with. For their votes, legislators (being wily, tactful and practical men) much preferred cash, but when cash could not be fingered, they conveniently took whatever "inducements" were offered. We have come across instance after instance in which embryo capitalists organized corporations, rolled off stocks and bonds (which cost the expense of engraving only) and used them, in lieu of cash, as payment for legislative votes.

If the average railroad corporation, argued the Pacific quartet, could so easily, by the simple media of bought laws, annex itself to public treasuries, what could not they do? A far more telling and impressive public argument the Huntington group had than most of their fellow railroad promoters. Already "in the fifties" there was an insistent, genuinely enthusiastic popular demand, reaching almost the proportions of a clamor, for railroad connections between coast and coast. Upon the strength of this eagerness, much bounty and booty could be extracted. At the outbreak of the Civil War the demand became irresistibly intensified by the lack of speedy intercoastal communications, both railroad and telegraph. Moreover, the popular imagination was captivated and dazzled by the immensity of the undertaking. With prevailing opinion in so favorably an assenting state, matters could be pliably molded.

Yet while the people, as a whole, were desirous of Pacific railroads, considerable sections of them were by no means reconciled to the corrupt legislative methods of presenting large areas of land and large advances of money for private enrichment.

The farmer, burdened by the price that he had to pay for his small farm, and often blanketed by a mortgage, did not quite approve of the squandering of the public domain for the benefit of a law-created handful of grandees. The small traders, resenting the very idea of any class above them, bitterly objected, as a class, to great capitalists being created by virtual edict of law. The alert and organized sections of the working class saw in this constant manipulation of legislative bodies another perversion of governmental power for the aggrandizement of a small and hostile class, and the rapid impetus to an overshadowing plutocracy. Aware of this general feeling, legislative assemblies had to be "induced"; they might themselves use fine-sounding and seemingly solid arguments in explaining to constituencies; but a very different incentive appealed to them; settlements had to be made in cash or its equivalent.

A more temptingly opportune time for spoliative measures than the period of the Civil War could hardly have been found. Engrossed in the tumultuous upheavals of those convulsive years, the people had neither the patience nor disposition to keep close track of routine enactments in Congress or in the legislatures. At the very beginning of that war the Huntington group organized the Central Pacific Railroad Company, with a capital stock of $8,500,000, nearly the whole of which capital was fictitious so far as actual investment of money was concerned. At once they directed their energies right to the core of things. Huntington betook himself to Washington to lobby in Congress, while Stanford, elected Governor of California, busied himself with similar ends at home. No visionaries were they, but practical men who knew how to proceed straightway.

Stanford's work quickly bore fruit in California; the city of Sacramento was authorized to donate $400,000; Placer County to loan $550,000, and the State of California to hand over $2,100,000. At the same time, Huntington was doing surpassing missionary duty in Congress. An act was passed in 1862 by which about $25,000,000 in Government six-per-cent. bonds and about 4,500,000 acres of public lands were placed at the disposal of the quartet. The few protests against these great gifts were immediately silenced. "Is not the Government fully protected?" the promoters innocently inquired. "Are not its loans covered by a first mortgage? If the company defaults, cannot the Government step in and recover?" This sounded plausible. Two years later, however, at the very time when . . . the Union Pacific coterie were corrupting Congress to get greater land grants and altered laws, Huntington again debauched Congress. An act was passed doubling the Central Pacific's land grant and relegating the Government's claim on the Central Pacific to the under position of a second mortgage. And, as it turned out later, the contract with the Government was so deftly drawn that, according to a decision of the Supreme Court of the United States subsequently, the Government's lien covered the main lines only, and not the branch lines. Whether this contract, as drawn, was a result of collusion with Government officials was never determined.

"Whence came the means," asks Bancroft, "by which four men with only moderate fortunes were enabled to build, buy, own and operate all the roads belonging to the Central and Southern Pacific systems? In 1869, before the last spike had been driven at Promontory, the railroad quartet, besides owning the road, had received as a loan $24,000,000 of Government bonds forming a second mortgage on the road, together with $400,000 of San Francisco bonds as an unconditional gift, $550,000 of county bonds, and $2,100,000 paid, or to be paid, by the State of California in return for services to be rendered by the company."

The operations of the quartet were simple enough. Once they had obtained the requisite loans and gifts, they threw aside all pretenses, and openly and vigorously set out to defraud all within reach, not only the Federal Government, but also States, counties, cities and investors. First, they organized a construction company, called the Credit and Finance Company. Then they made a contract with themselves to build the Central Pacific. With the aid of the loans given by Sacramento and Placer County, they built enough road to draw $848,000 from the Government as the subsidy of the first section. By repeating the process they had the entire road constructed, with scarcely the expenditure of a single dollar of their own. The next step was to load it down with a capitalization of $139,000,000 which was the beginning of still more stock inflation. . . .

The process of corruption and theft was continued in the building of the Southern Pacific Railroad.

In 1871 Congress chartered the Texas

and Pacific Railroad to run from Marshall, Texas, to San Diego, Cal., and presented the company with approximately 18,000,000 acres of public lands on condition that the road was to be completed in ten years; otherwise the land grant was to be declared forfeited. At the same time, Congress chartered the Southern Pacific Railroad Company to build a line from El Paso, Texas, to San Francisco, and gave it a gift of about 5,000,000 acres of public lands. The Texas and Pacific project was owned by a group of capitalists headed by Scott, of the Pennsylvania Railroad; the Huntington men were at the head of the Southern Pacific Railroad Company.

These two groups of capitalists soon came into collision; each fiercely sought to oust the other, and gain an undisputed monopoly of transportation in the territory in question. The fight was carried into Congress; each side caused the introduction of bills aimed at crippling the other. The contest then narrowed to a question of which group could corrupt Congress the more effectually.

"Scott," wrote Huntington on January 29, 1876, "is making a terrible effort to pass his bill, and he has many advantages with his railroad running out from Washington in almost every direction, on which he gives Free Passes to everyone who can help him ever so little. . . . It has cost money to fix things, so I know his bill would not pass. I believe with $200,000 we can pass our bill."

On March 6, 1876, Huntington wrote that "the Railroad Committee of the House was set up for Scott, and it has been a very difficult matter to switch a majority of the Committee from him, but I think it has been done." On November 11, 1876, Huntington wrote further to one of his associates, "I am glad to learn that you will send to this office $2,000,000 by the first of January." On May 3, 1878, he notified his partners: "The T. and P. folks are working hard on their bill and say they are sure to pass it, but I do not believe it. They offered one member of Congress $1,000 cash down, $5,000 when the bill was passed and $10,000 of the bonds when they got them if he would vote for the bill."

Huntington came out victorious. "There is no room for doubt," reported the Pacific Railroads Commission of 1887, "that a large portion of $4,818,535 was used for the purpose of influencing legislation, and preventing the passage of measures deemed hostile to the interests of the company, for the purpose of influencing elections."

The next thing the Huntington group did was to force the Eastern capitalists out of the Texas and Pacific Railroad, absorb that line into their own system, and illegally grab the eighteen million-acre land grant of the Texas and Pacific. Even under the law, as it stood, the Texas and Pacific was not entitled to the land grant. The House Committee on Judiciary on August 3, 1882, after an investigation, declared that the Texas and Pacific Railroad Company had never completed any part of the route for which the land grant in New Mexico, Arizona and California was given; that it "had never earned the grant"; that it did not purpose to build

the road for which it was chartered and endowed, and that it was transferring to the Southern Pacific Railroad Company "all of the rights and titles to the land in question." The Committee on Judiciary prepared a resolution declaring the forfeiture of the land grant, and urged its passage by Congress as a joint resolution. It did not pass.

Presenting the general results as nearly as official investigations could ascertain them, this is what Huntington and his associates did: They had received hundreds of millions of dollars in the form of money, bonds and lands from Government, States, counties and municipalities. As controllers of the Contract and Finance Company and other construction companies, they had turned over to themselves $142,000,000 in all for ostensible construction work. They had expended at least five millions for corrupt political purposes. They had stupendously watered the stock of their railroads, and with the cumulative proceeds of their thefts had secured control of nineteen distinct railway systems and of steamship lines, also. They had, by fraud, robbed the Government of many millions of acres of land; they had defrauded the Government of the bulk of the funds that it had advanced; they refused to pay more than the merest nominal taxation, and they extorted onerous rates for transporation.

DAVID J. ROTHMAN (b. 1937), an associate professor of history at Columbia University, in his book *Politics and Power: The United States Senate, 1869–1901* (1966) challenges the corrupt nature of Gilded Age politics as expressed by Myers. The Senate reigned as the dominant house where most bills received final form, but Rothman holds that senators were not "kept men" on the payroll of various corporations. He claims that in this period the Senate assumed its modern character, which rests on party machinery and leadership, and he demonstrates that the moguls could not rely on the Senate to do their bidding. In addition to the heterogeneity of business interests, Rothman attributes the unpredictability of Senate actions to the lack of sophistication in the embryonic lobbying structure.*

David J. Rothman

The Indecisiveness of Political Influence

Various interest groups in post-Civil War America attempted to manipulate political power. Although laissez-faire doctrines undoubtedly carried some appeal, still, as James Bryce remarked in 1888: "The lamentations with which old-fashioned English thinkers accompany the march of legislation, are in America scarcely heard and wholly unheeded." Americans, he believed, customarily welcomed "the action of government into ever-widening fields." In fact the people were probably too busy devising intricate schemes for the legislature to spare the time for complaint. Laissez-faire theories notwithstanding, the voters assumed that abstract intellectual commitments would not prevent an institution like the Senate from acting, provided the pressures exerted were great enough.

Although various associations appeared in Washington during these years, the business groups rather than the farmers, or the laborers, or the consumers most diligently attempted to influence politics. Their efforts, more than any others, at once shaped and were affected by the place of party in government. Since no particular enterprise could wield power in several state legislatures and campaign contributions did not guarantee favorable action, companies turned to other expedients, especially lobbying. Still the results were not to their liking; corporations could not dictate political decisions. As the most relentless pursuers of power,

*From David J. Rothman, *Politics and Power: The United States Senate, 1869–1901.* Cambridge, Mass.: Harvard University Press, Copyright, 1966, by the President and Fellows of Harvard College. Pp. 191–203. Footnotes omitted.

their fate clarified some of the implications of the Senate's transformation.

In the 1870's, when party did not yet superintend the course of Senate affairs, lobbying for the first time became a vital element in government. In initial appearance, however, lobbyists were careless and haphazard, neither especially benefiting nor endangering Senate proceedings. The cause of the disorganization rested not with the agents but with their chief sponsors, the railroads. Transporation companies were by no means unique in their Washington practices—many midwestern towns with a creek hoped to promⱬte a canal that would empty into the Mississippi—but they were lobbying's most devoted patrons. Some lines energetically tried to capture congressional appropriations while others were equally determined to maintain privileges. But whatever their goals, they could not systematically pursue them without help.

The railroads in the 1870's were critically short of money. Collis Huntington, president of the Central Pacific and the Southern Pacific, lacked sufficient funds to fulfill numerous construction plans and still he was far wealthier than Tom Scott of the Texas & Pacific. The need for capital in business ventures left little room for political expenditures just as it made government assistance all the more necessary. Begrudging every cost, executives frugally doled out their money and intently watched for the return on their investment.

The results of the railroad's economies were apparent in the early career of William Chandler. After the Civil War, the New Hampshire Republican opened a one-man lobbying firm, without an office or staff. Typical of his profession, Chandler accepted employment from a startling number of companies and even from competing organizations. Until the mid-

1880's he served as chief lobbyist for the Union Pacific Railroad. "You will report frequently," charged Grenville Dodge, head engineer and sometime lobbyist, "to the proper officers of the Company, and will, of course, consult and advise on important matters, with any associate counsel . . . but in the absence of direction otherwise . . . your action will be authoritative." While exercising this warrant, Chandler accepted retainers from the Baltimore & Ohio, the Kansas Pacific, and the Atchinson, Topeka & Santa Fe, paying no attention to one company's friendships or another's rivalries.

Soon after the Northern Pacific was incorporated, Chandler also sought to take a part in its affairs. "Of course, we do not want you or anyone else to be antagonistic in this great work," responded the head of the line, Jay Cooke. "I am not willing to deprive you of a good fee, if our Company had no objections." Chandler was hired and soon intervening for Cooke's interests in Union Pacific affairs. Finally in 1873, when Tom Scott began his long but unsuccessful attempt to win congressional underwriting for his railroad's bonds, Chandler joined his old friend Dodge as a Texas & Pacific lobbyist. Although the Union Pacific did not always smile on Scott's enterprise, he readily served both companies.

Lobbyists accepted numerous and conflicting retainers, for few employers paid satisfactory fees. In 1869 Chandler received only $5,000 in return for several years' service on behalf of the Union Pacific, and in 1870 he was forced to accept stock when the road could not, or would not, pay cash. Estimating his total 1871 income from lobbying at a meager $3,000, Chandler furiously denounced Union Pacific president Oliver Ames for begrudging the agents every cent of their salaries. Moreover, financial prospects did not improve in time. "I am $5000 dollars worse off than I was one year ago," he complained to Dodge in 1873, and it was small consolation to learn that the line was niggardly with other lobbyists as well.

Collis Huntington and other company presidents would not divulge political expenses, lumping them under "legal costs" on the books, but the scorn they heaped on the lobbyists was unlimited and unconcealed. "The damned strikers are so numerous," lamented Huntington to his partners in 1870, "that if we should endeavor to put the matter [of purchasing government property in San Francisco's harbor] before Congress this session I have no doubt it would cost us more than it would be worth . . . The Strikers, or Third House members, are very quick and hungry in Washington this winter." Seven years later conditions and attitudes had not changed appreciably. "It seems as though all the strikers in the world" were gathered in Washington. "If we are not hurt this session," Huntington irritably contended, "it will be because we pay much money to prevent it, and you know how hard it is to get it to pay for such purposes."

Nevertheless, when the Southern Pacific and Texas & Pacific were urging rival proposals before Congress, Huntington was afraid to forego help. Partner Mark Hopkins suggested hiring a certain lobbyist, and the railroad president immediately agreed. "I should not want to pay him a great price for I do not believe Scott can pass his bill," he lamely added, "but I think it of so much importance to us that I do not want it to fail for any lack on our own part." In fact, Charles Crocker, another associate, found Huntington overcautious. "I would not spend a dollar to beat Tom Scott," he told his colleague in 1878, "for I think he is al-

ready beaten without it. You are there, where the lobby has access to you, and their bread and butter depends upon their making themselves seem necessary to the success of any movement." Of course, matters were not very different for Tom Scott. One would-be lobbyist was informed that although he could be "of great service to Scott's Texas railroad bill . . . money is scarce everywhere." The company, however, would "allow . . . $50 per week for expenses, for a month anyway, possibly for the session." Employers were even more trying than congressmen.

Lobbyists also required substantial sums to cover their costs. "There [are] a lot of Press fellows here who are after us unless we pay," Richard Franchot, a Southern Pacific agent in Washington, noted frankly in 1872. Hotels, entertainment, cigars, and champagne were other drains, especially when supporters traveled to the capital and defended the corporation before Congress. Expenses climbed higher since Huntington, convinced that elected officials were attentive to constituents' telegrams and letters, detailed men to arrange writing campaigns. Then too, county and state resolutions could be still more effective. When the railroad president discovered that Scott, spending liberally, "gets every little gathering in the South to pass resolutions favoring the Texas & Pacific bill," he immediately set out to emulate him. Naturally, efforts in Washington often had to be duplicated in state legislatures. Federalism insured that all attempts to influence politics would be extraordinarily expensive.

The narrow-minded president of the Southern Pacific devised three special categories for public men: the clean, the commercial, and the communists. Huntington's finest compliment was to label a politician clean. "Sargent has done all we have asked, and is an able and honest man," began his description of the California Congressman who subsequently won election to the Senate. "He is a very clean man and will do the right all the time." Short of capital and loathe to spend it, the California entrepreneur highly valued any senator who would consistently do the right without seeking favors in return. For these very select few, he reserved the title clean. Next, but lower, in his estimation were the commercial—officials, whose support was purchasable. "Scott is working mostly amongst the commercial men," Huntington informed head lobbyist David Colton in 1876. "He switched Senator Spencer of Alabama and Walker of Virginia this week, but you know they can be switched back with the 'proper arguments' when they are wanted." Proper arguments called for the expenditure of funds, but at least commercial politicians were tractable. Huntington despaired only of the communists. They combated his pet projects incessantly and could not be dissuaded by the strongest of arguments or the handsomest of gifts.

The handful of clean senators were not neglected by their admirer. "If you could," the railroad man instructed partner Leland Stanford on the subject of Roscoe Conkling, "arrange something out of which he could make some money (something handsome). You will have to be very careful how you do it, as he is very sensitive, but, of course, like the rest of us, has to eat and drink." Because the New Yorker was "so straight he leans backwards," he was not to be "deprived of this world's goods." Senators William Stewart and Samuel Pomeroy were also gratuitously rewarded, and as for Sargent, "he is," proclaimed Huntington, "our friend, without doubt, but we must

take care of our friends." Even when John Conness, a "good and true friend" of the enterprise was defeated for Senate re-election, he was not abandoned to his own devices. "He has a large family of children . . . and I think we should do something handsome for him," the company president instructed his colleagues. "He should have something handsome; something worth from six to ten thousand dollars a year . . . He is not the man to beg of us or any one else, but I think we owe it."

These supporters, of course, were thanked without any direct cash expenditure. Conness was tendered a job with the company, Conkling was offered "an interest in some city or town property on the line of the road," Sargent received company stock, and Stewart was granted "fifty thousand acres of land of average quality of the lands along the line of the road." Although such gifts might hopefully insure the steadfastness of a loyalty, Huntington did not intend to corrupt public officials. In fact, he instructed his partners not to inform Conkling and Pomeroy of the arrangements, for "they would take nothing from us while they are in Congress."

In December 1883 the alleged corruption spread by the railroads provoked a public furor second only in its intensity to Credit Mobilier. After the death of chief lobbyist David Colton, his widow, dissatisfied with her property settlement, sued the Southern Pacific. She introduced Huntington's letters to his top-Washington contact into evidence, and straightway they were reprinted prominently in the country's newspapers. When reporters interviewed him about the correspondence, Huntington, without embarrassment, expressed amazement at the excitement. "Where's the evidence of corruption in these?" he demanded. "I've been in business fifty years and practiced the usual methods known among business men to accomplish certain objects, but I've never bought votes or bribed men directly or indirectly." The materials themselves lent some support to his contention, and a later congressional investigatory board exonerated him from the charges. In 1876, during the fierce battle with Scott, for example, Huntington confessed to Mark Hopkins that he might have won over certain congressmen to the road "had they not been offered large sums" to vote against him. "You know our rule is never to buy a vote." He also expressed similar sentiments to Colton himself; Scott promised to pay huge sums, but "you know I keep on the high ground."

Although the Southern Pacific president halfheartedly denied in congressional examinations that "commercial Congressmen" designated men willing to be bribed, he ultimately conceded the venality of some officeholders. "Eighteen hundred years ago," Huntington reminded his questioners, "the best man that ever lived selected twelve men and 16⅔ per cent of them were 'short weight.'" A few politicians might be influenced by money, "and while it is very likely that there have always been such men in Congress," still it never helped to traffic with them. The dangers of discovery and scandal were great, and buying two or three officials drove away ten honest men. He might have added, but it demanded too much candor, that a vote purchased by one bidder could easily be won over by another; then too, the strategy was too expensive to adopt as a habitual practice. Occasionally a supporter could be picked up with a generous gift—short weight men we have always with us—but economic interests did not influence the political process through bribery.

Most senators did not fit into any of Huntington's ingenious classifications, and corporation presidents perceived that an overwhelming majority of the chamber was neither steadfastly in favor of, nor unalterably opposed to, their pet projects. A few determined supporters and detractors were often on hand; nevertheless, the fate of legislation rested with a large, diverse, and uncommitted membership. On this unattached bloc, the companies exerted their funds and energies, compelled to convince individual senators of a proposal's validity. Despite the great cost of the effort, the results remained unpredictable.

The purpose of lobbying, declared Huntington, was to gain a full and sympathetic congressional hearing; since elected officials were most attentive to a constituent or an acquaintance, business interests thought it most effective to locate and retain men "whom he [the congressman] would allow to talk to him." If a single agent could have fulfilled the corporations' purposes, they would willingly have allowed him a satisfactory retainer. But the California entrepreneur and his rivals were required to hire part-time, one-session lobbyists who, having access to one or two congressmen by some chance, for a fee were willing to expound the virtues of a particular design. Huntington accurately estimated that in the winter of 1876–77, Tom Scott employed some two hundred lobbyists in Washington. Each would corner a few politicians and explain Texas & Pacific contentions. No one particular salary was large but the size of the payroll made the total outlay enormous.

As Scott discovered, a flock of agents was no guarantee of satisfaction; his line never did win congressional backing. Arguments could be countered; the men lobbyists exhorted were soon visited by rivals. To bring a measure of stability to the chaos, companies often attempted to capture good will as well as intellectual agreement. An obligation might be repaid with a loyal vote. Although bribery was neither permissible nor desirable, there were other methods for bestowing favors on potential supporters.

Corporations willingly advanced loans to men in office. The maneuver was legally defensible, albeit on weak moral grounds; more important, the funds did not necessarily determine the borrower's actions. When California first sent Cornelius Cole to the Senate in 1865, Huntington, convinced "he is much the best for us," was happy with the choice. Within two years, however, he altered his opinion. "There is no good feeling in Cole," he bitterly warned his colleagues; "his heart is cold and his blood is white and I do not nor cannot like him." Yet Cole owned a vote and when he requested a loan, the railroad agreed. Cole had promised to "do all that he could for us," the president now assured his partners. Still the Senator did not reliably support the road; the favor did not secure his loyalty. When Cole was finally defeated for reelection in 1873, Huntington quickly wrote to Hopkins: "Herewith I send you account and some notes against Cornelius Cole. He has often promised to pay them . . . [but] he did not. You will collect these notes and accounts, if you can do so." When Cole was tardy with his payments, Huntington wished to sue him. At least *one* bad investment would be recovered.

The Texas & Pacific followed identical practices with as little success. When Georgia senator John Gordon needed $5,000, he turned to one of their lobbyists, Sam Barlow; two others admittedly had offered him the money, but, he told Barlow, "you would not consent to my taking the loan from either as long as I am in the Senate, did you know the sources." Gordon believed that he could take funds from the Texas & Pacific lobbyist with impunity, and when the Scott bill was raised in the chamber, the Senator informed his benefactor: "I cannot vote for it. There is nothing as you know which I could do consistently, at which I would hesitate to oblige you; but not only my convictions but my constituents are against it . . . I know you would not have me guilty of a shadow of turning from my convictions on any matter of legislation." Good will did not always insure roll-call support, and many senators were willing to accept gifts precisely because they did not feel bound to repay them on the Senate floor. Corporations' best laid plans often found their proverbial endings.

The distribution of railroad passes to congressmen began as another stratagem to win supporters, but demand soon overwhelmed willingness to supply, the business organizations found themselves making more enemies than friends. The roads were expected to issue passes, and recipients felt no obligation to repay the favor; but, at the same time, those denied the courtesy took offense. Since they could ill afford to provoke more antagonism, company heads were as opposed to the system as any Granger legislature. "When in Washington," Huntington informed Mark Hopkins in 1869, "I had to give out many passes, mostly at the request of Senators and Members of Congress, and since Congress adjourned I think we have averaged six letters per day from Senators and Members of Congress asking for passes over the road. I refuse many, and I give many. This giving free passes is all wrong."

Nevertheless, the pressure continued unabated. Vowing in 1870 to refuse passes to all "except those that I am quite sure can and will help us," Huntington angrily reminded Stanford five years later that the Central Pacific had carried 6,186 deadheads, "which is a fearful number to carry free on a road like the Central . . . I think we made a mistake three times out of four in issuing passes." But many senators' requests, not very subtly, mentioned the speed and generosity with which a rival line met their demands, and companies would not allow competitors even the most dubious advantages. Passes remained bothersome and expensive, not effective corrupters of public officials.

Railroads also sold congressmen stock at very attractive prices and placed their relatives in sinecures somewhere on the payroll. Yet even those most handsomely treated repeatedly failed to back the organization at the crucial times. Aaron Sargent was one of the few "clean" public men, at least until 1875 when for no obvious reason he turned "very cross and bitter against the Central Pacific Railroad people," and resigned his strategic position on the Senate Railroad Commitee. "His going off," observed Huntington, "looks as if he did not care to help us or harm us much." During the next year, Sargent became even more "bitter, and very active," and "if necessary," it seemed, "would sit up all night to do us harm." With bewildering inconsistency, however, he once again shifted course, and in 1877 Huntington gleefully reported: "I have had a talk with Sargent. He will be all right and I think we would be better off with him in the Senate than with almost any one else." Senators, corporations discovered, were not loyal allies. They deserve rebuke for accepting the companies' gifts, and the companies deserve censure for having offered them. Yet it must not be forgotten that whatever corruption existed did not settle the fate of legislative questions.

Despite significant expenditures and efforts, from the most legitimate to the most questionable, business interests could not efficiently prejudice the legislative process. Their methods were too haphazard. Reviewing the events of these decades, Huntington confided to a California friend: "We have never had any men in Congress—either branch—with the exception of three, that have been worth anything to the State or to ourselves." And a lobbyist, named Taylor, for the Texas & Pacific, told Sam Barlow that the road's failure to win its way in Congress was due to a want of organization and to misdirected ventures in Washington. "The measure had every element of success, equity, sectional feeling, local interests, hostility to Huntington and Gould, politics." But because of ineptitude, "all have been frittered away." The numerous lobbyists so frequently worked at cross purposes and accomplished nothing that Taylor despaired of the whole system. "There should be one man here with full powers who should have no dealing save with Senators and Congressmen," he recommended. "It is a waste of money to attempt anything in the future without an organization inside of both Houses of Congress. Lobbyists are positively detrimental." The company had squandered "time and money after shadows."

These judgments by Huntington and Taylor were not official cant designed to mislead a naive public. Rather, they represented considered and accurate opinions. Lobbying, as its practitioners fully understood, was not an effective political tool. The costs were high and the returns unreliable. Other methods did not guarantee any better results. Companies were by no means scrupulous in their dealings, but dishonesty was not necessarily rewarded. Loans, gifts, jobs, and railroad passes did not effectively determine political decisions.

It is no simple matter to explain why

a legislature acted as it did. In light of the public's reaction against the railroads, for example, congressional legislation in the 1870's might have been more drastic. But although the government did not cripple the lines, it certainly did not deal with them generously. Rather than capturing new land grants, companies faced forfeitures, sinking fund requirements, and rate regulation. These decisions resulted from a long series of congressional estimates and deliberations; they were not simple reflex actions to the hammer of business interests. The corporations' efforts were too muddled and their agents too unskilled to deserve any credit—and the companies themselves shared this conclusion. Lobbyists frequently warned their boss to "get your house in order," for it might well "snow or hail or rain." If corporations manipulated congressional politics so effectively, why did company presidents celebrate adjournments, thankful that the enterprise had survived?

Business interests during these years faced a Senate of individuals, not of well organized parties, and the dispersal of energies heightened the confusion. Political consolidation would soon reorder the institution, but the alterations would only increase the difficulties.

FRITZ REDLICH (b. 1892), professor emeritus at Harvard University, is best known for his monumental *The Molding of American Banking: Men and Ideas* (2 vols.; 1948, 1952). During the 1950s he was closely associated with Harvard's Research Center in Entrepreneurial History. In the following selection Redlich claims that black-white interpretations fail to appreciate that the mogul was both creative and destructive. Agreeing for the most part with economist Joseph Schumpeter, he concludes that the robber baron doomed himself as a permanent fixture in American society not because of his ruthlessness but rather "because of his creative achievements. . . ." He also offers an explanation, though not a defense, of the businessman's conduct during the Gilded Age. Does Redlich's "consensus" approach sound more plausible than the extreme critics and defenders of the robber barons?*

Fritz Redlich

The Robber Baron:
Creative and Destructive

Whenever a major phenomenon has two such contradictory aspects as has that of the business leader, the superficial observer will be inclined to stress the one and to forget the other. This is exactly what has been done in our field, and we have descriptions stressing the destructive aspect of entrepreneurship on the one hand, and highly laudatory presentations on the other. The former type of literature is usually called "muckraking." Beginning in McClure's era it has come to contain such works as Henry Demarest Lloyd's *Wealth Against Commonwealth* (1894), Ida Tarbell's *History of the Standard Oil Company* (which began to appear in 1902), Gustavus Myer's *History of American Fortunes* (1909–1910), and many other works, including recently

those of Anna Rochester. The laudatory type, on the other hand, consists of the numerous authorized and possibly paid-for biographies of businessmen such as Ida Tarbell's biography of Judge Gary (1925), Satterlee's biography of Morgan (1939), Anna R. Burr's biography of Stillman (1927), and so on.

It goes without saying that neither kind of presentation is tenable, since neither gives a balanced picture. A correct history or analysis of business leadership must combine both the creative and the destructive aspects thereof, and a tool to that end is suggested in Paul Tillich's concept of the DAIMONIC. Going beyond Tillich's own interpretation of this term the author proposes that it be made to convey two meanings: He will

*From "The Business Leader as a 'Daimonic' Figure," *The American Journal of Economics and Sociology*, XII (1953), January-April, 163–176, 289–299.

speak of the daimonic to denote the fact that in the economic field hardly any real creation is possible without concomitant destruction, or in other words, the fact that destruction results from the creative act as such, because "the destructive power is essentially connected with [the] creative power." But economic institutions, like others, are daimonic also in the sense that destruction may "not come from without, [may] not depend on deficiency or powerlessness" but may "originate from the basis of the form itself," as Professor Tillich has phrased it. In David Hume's words, "there is no constitution of human fabric but what engenders in itself the seed for its own destruction."

Of these two phenomena, the former may be designated as daimonic destructiveness, the latter as daimonic self-destructiveness, both of which have to be distinguished clearly from destructiveness and self-destructiveness, which are not daimonic in character since they do not stem from creativity, but from weakness or wickedness. Professor Tillich has made it clear that the daimonic receives power and comes to fulfillment only in personalities, so that it is meaningful, indeed, to speak of the business leader as a daimonic figure. It is he in whom is lodged that "creative-destructive" power which can be seen at work in the economic field.

Professor Schumpeter, in characterizing the capitalistic process as one of "creative destruction," has pointed to the very phenomenon that is here called daimonic. He has described that process as "incessantly revolutionizing the economic structure from within, incessantly destroying the old one, incessantly erecting a new one."

Such revolutions result each time in "avalanches of consumers goods that permanently deepen and widen the stream of real income, although in the first instances they spell disturbances, losses and unemployment." The introduction of the power loom, to give an example, destroyed the hand weaver's craft. It did so *ipso facto;* and every new labor-saving device tended in the same direction, until after the destruction of all hand crafts, it came to result "only" in technological unemployment.

The capitalistic process, "not by coincidence, but by virtue of its mechanism, progressively raises the standard of life of the masses . . . through sequences of vicissitudes the severity of which is proportionate to the speed of the advance." Moreover, inventions, if introduced into the business practice in the form of new capital equipment, annihilate, or at least reduce, the value of previously used capital. They make it obsolete, although from the technological point of view it could perhaps serve for many more years. The so-called "scrap heap policy," devised in Andrew Carnegie's enterprise at a period in which "monopolistic" practices did not prevail as yet, was the result and an expression of our highly dynamic "creative-destructive" economic system.

Finally, shifts of industrial locations due to the creative processes of building up large scale industry or of moving to better sources of raw material, centers of labor supply, and the like, result in the destruction of existing plants and enterprises and may directly or indirectly hit whole communities which decay or even become ghost towns.

These are but a few examples of the cost of capitalistic "progress;" it proceeds over roads strewn with corpses and wreckage, shocking evidences of what is called here daimonic destructiveness.

Up to now, in order to make use of

Schumpeter's analysis, we have adopted the term capitalistic "process." But the bearers of this process are, of course, "creative entrepreneurs" who in this context must be characterized properly as "creative-destructive" or daimonic.

Of course, daimonic destructiveness in the field of business is nothing recent. It made its appearance at the very moment in which the creative entrepreneur (the innovating business leader) entered the scene in the era of early capitalism. When after the Industrial Revolution he became active in one field after another, daimonic destructiveness was bound to play a larger and larger role; but it did not become perceptible to superficial observers of economic life before the era of the Robber Barons. To be sure, not even then was it understood.

The term Robber Barons, as is generally known, was coined by Carl Schurz who used it to denote the destructive aspect of contemporaneous big business. The businessmen whom he had in mind, the Rockefellers, Morgans, Carnegies, etc., the leaders predominant in the later years of Schurz's life, were mostly born between about 1835 and 1845: namely,

Jim Fisk	1834
Peter A. B. Widener	1834
Andrew Carnegie	1835
Jay Gould	1836
Charles Tyson Yerkes	1837
J. P. Morgan	1837
James Keene	1838
James J. Hill	1838
John D. Rockefeller	1839
H. H. Rogers	1840
George F. Baker	1840
William Rockefeller	1841
William C. Whitney	1841
George F. Baer	1842

The author is convinced that this coincidence of birth years of the men, who regardless of all differences bear a similarity in essentials, is no accident. He feels that those whom Carl Schurz denoted as "Robber Barons" represented, in fact, a "group of coevals," and that the sudden appearance of an unusual degree of both destructiveness and daimonic destructiveness in the decades following the Civil War was a generation phenomenon.

The theory of generations, to which the author has just made allusion, was developed in this century by several European scholars, especially Eduard Wechssler. According to this theory, men who are born within a nation during a given span of time assume for the rest of their lives certain characteristic ways of thinking, attitudes, and behavior patterns which distinguish them from people who are born as members of the same nation in somewhat earlier or later decades.

Such decisive characteristics are acquired because, as a matter of course, men born in certain years grow up during a certain span of time; or to put it differently, their most impressionable age falls into certain periods. As adolescents and young men, *i.e.*, between the ages of about 15 and 25, they are impressed by and react on the economic, social, political, intellectual, and religious situation of that period which they experience in common. To make it clear beyond doubt, it is not the year of their birth, but the years of their adolescence and early manhood which determine the mental frame of men.

The social, economic, etc. situation of a time presents to the men who mature in this time a set of problems and tasks; it leads to a community of problems and tasks, not to a community of goals, and even less to a community of solutions. It goes without saying that there is an overlapping at the borderlines of generations, but to analyze this here would go beyond the scope of this paper. . . .

Details cannot be discussed in this paper; but it seems to the author that the Robber Barons, or in other words, the American business leaders born between about 1835 and 1845 possess that remarkable similarity of thinking, attitudes, and behavior patterns which is typical of groups of coevals. The foremost determining event for this particular generation was the Civil War. The problem which it posed, and which those members of the generation who became businessmen had to master, was that of mass production and the concomitant building of large-scale enterprise.

The technological stage was set when this group of coevals started out by about 1860. Its members saw business possibilities and, making use of them, very successfully gave the answer to the burning problem of their day. By this becoming creative they were bound to become destructive; a high degree of daimonic destructiveness was their fate, since theirs was a highly creative achievement. But, in fact, they became more destructive than would have been unavoidable because of certain ideas which they had absorbed when young and because of certain attitudes which they shared as members of their group of coevals.

Here then it is possible to study the dividing line between destructiveness and daimonic destructiveness, a dividing line which Schumpeter has seen in a somewhat different context when he investigated the destruction of "protecting strata" by the capitalistic process; the latter, as he remarked, wrought destruction much beyond what was necessary.

The majority of the business leaders of the generation of the Robber Barons were church members and church goers, and it would be totally erroneous to consider them as hypocrites. They felt themselves to be on very good terms with their God, and they were, according to their lights, religious and righteous men. Thus one could expect a minimum of avoidable destructiveness. That, in spite of all this, many of their deeds, *i.e.*, many of their business transactions, went far beyond daimonic destructiveness, and were far from being in line with Christian ethics must be explained.

The Calvinist creed of the American as well as of the European brand, in contrast to Lutheran religiosity, had in the preceding centuries always been reflected in daily life. In order to understand that phenomenon we must remember that Puritanism, to which most of them adhered, was strongly influenced by the Old Testament, whose ethics are different from New Testament ethics. Moreover, the influence of Biblical ethics on the generation of the Robber Barons was on the wane; it was competing with other systems of thought, the destructive aspects of which are obvious. Such ideas were the laissez-faire and the natural law concepts and the acceptance of competition as ordained by God; (competition as such tends to be warlike and destructive, of course).

To make things worse, not only were religious checks wearing out during the lifetime of the Robber Barons, but also such other checks as had kept earlier generations of businessmen in bounds. Such checks had been custom and "perfect" (atomistic) competition of what one may call the classical type.

In the era of large-scale enterprises, working with a high percentage of fixed capital, competition would not be beneficial and would not work as the classical economists envisaged. To the contrary, it would easily become so destructive that for the benefit of all concerned and, in fact, for the benefit of the national economy, it had to be abandoned, and actually was over wide areas. But the check which competition had exerted before, disappeared *ipso facto* also, while government, as a regulator, had not entered the scene as yet.

On the whole . . . the generation of the Robber Barons was lacking a sense for social and national responsibility (a lack which made for avoidable destructiveness) and a distinctly negative attitude toward government. Both characteristics were rooted in their concept of an autonomous, self-adjusting economy, as Professor Cochran puts it. That group of coevals could not see how government could have any important function in economic life, unless business called on it, and its members could never understand that their own irresponsible and destructive actions called it onto the scene. Destructiveness thus turned into self-destructiveness. The attitude of these men toward government, an attitude which became dominant for decades to come, ranged all the way from indifference to outright contempt.

Untrammelled by checks, the creative business leaders of the late nineteenth century built up modern large-scale enterprise, and they used the corporate mechanism to that end. Its application opened up tremendous profit chances without there being a direct connection with the production or distribution of goods and services. . . .

Turning now to the self-destructiveness of business leaders, we venture the suggestion that it is due, to a large extent, to persistence of ways of thinking, attitudes, and behavior patterns which had once contributed to creative achievements. Guided by this hypothesis, we will study first certain ways of thinking, attitudes, and behavior patterns of businessmen which are to the point.

We shall discuss self-destructiveness of businessmen which is due to weakness, but since that weakness became weakness only as the result of previous achievements, the concept of the daimonic provides the explanation. We are going to meet the problem which Toynbee calls the "nemesis of creativity," a phenomenon which undoubtedly belongs in the realm of the daimonic: once certain behavior patterns have led to success it is almost impossible for those originally benefited thereby to abandon them until it is too late.

To understand that statement and others which will be made later, it must be kept in mind that human history, and especially *Geistesgeschichte,* can be presented as a history of human errors. There has never been a time which was not ruled by ideas which later generations came to despise as absurd. Moreover there never was a civilization which did not experience behavior patterns which other civilizations considered, or that same civilization came to consider later, as cruelties or atrocities.

As long as errors are honestly believed in, as long as doubtful actions are sincerely considered fair, they are not necessarily dangerous to the institutions to which they refer or to the civilization which brought such ideas or behavior patterns into existence. When, on the other hand, previously-accepted errors or cruelties have come to be recognized as such by the advanced minds of a time or a civilization, they are bound to poison a period or even to blight a whole civilization unless they are discarded quickly.

This is true also with regard to ideas and behavior patterns which are correct only in relation to a specific institutional set-up. They too become not only untenable, but also destructive if the latter changes and they are not abandoned in time.

These general statements lead up to the specific assertion that in many cases ways of thinking, behavior patterns, and attitudes, which were not only not detrimental, but on the contrary, helpful to businessmen in one period became utterly dangerous for them in another.

None of them has become more dangerous to the future of the businessman than his irresponsibility. Although it has a long past, irresponsible behavior has become perilous only since the era of the Robber Barons when business leaders acquired that extraordinary power which will be studied later.

Irresponsibility of businessmen was originally rooted in the theory of laissez-faire. It will be remembered that the slogan of laissez-faire developed from the answer of a French merchant to Colbert. When the latter discussed with a group of merchants the possibility of developing French trade, their spokesman suggested "Laissez-nous faire," that is to say, he claimed that businessmen would be better able to promote French trade than government administrators. This claim to freedom of enterprise was made in a period which had embraced the belief in the harmony of the universe, the outstanding formulation of which is Leibniz's philosophy of a pre-established harmony.

From that root there grew the set of ideas which is so well known to economists, since it was embodied in the *Wealth of Nations*. To be sure, Adam Smith did not express anything new when he introduced the "invisible hand" into economics. According to Keynes "the idea of a divine harmony between private advantage and the public good [was] apparent" also in the writings of Archdeacon William Paley (1743–1805), especially in the widely read *Principles of Moral and Political Philosophy* of 1786.

But in fact this way of thinking must have been much older. As early as 1732 the thought can be found expressed in an American sermon in which the preacher stated: "A rich man is a great friend to the public while he aims at nothing but serving himself. God will have us live by helping one another, and since Love will not do it, Covetousness shall."

It is generally known that this type of thinking survived the eighteenth and persisted throughout the nineteenth century: In 1877, one hundred and fifty years after the above-quoted sermon, Samuel Tilden addressed a gathering of New York businessmen as follows: "You are, doubtless in some degree, clinging to the illusion that you are working for yourselves, but it is my pleasure to claim that you are working for the public. While you are scheming for your own selfish ends, there is an over-ruling and wise Providence directing that the most of all you do should inure to the benefit of the people. Men of colossal fortunes are in effect, if not in fact, trustees for the public."

It goes without saying that if a man honestly believes in the harmony of the social universe, if he honestly believes that God will take care that public interest evolves from the prosecution of private interests, he must not only believe in laissez-faire, but also has no reason to feel social or national responsibility for his actions. Express statements to the effect that businessmen and especially managers of corporations had no public responsibility can be found, for instance, in Condy Raguet's writings:

Banks are private speculations intended for profit and they are not called upon by any consideration of public duty any more than individuals are.

As time went on the belief in the "invisible hand" experienced changes in two different directions.

On the one hand it was secularized in typical nineteenth-century fashion. For the result Henry P. Davison, the Morgan partner, may be quoted. When asked by the counsel of the Pujo Committee if he could see an economic objection to a monopoly, he answered: "If in practice it were wrong it could not live . . . Things correct themselves." Or, to give another example, as late as 1949 Donald K. David, Dean of the Graduate School of Business Administration, Harvard University, wrote: "But we can be sure of this: the pendulum swings, and when it goes too far, it tends to adjust itself."

On the other hand, by the middle of the last century the belief in the "invisible hand" was replaced by a belief in the "natural law" as determining economic life. The effect of this change on businessmen's attitudes was bound to be nil; for again if a businessman is convinced that he is nothing but an agent through which the natural law works, he must, on the one hand, plead for laissez-faire and, on the other, cannot feel responsible for the repercussions of his actions. From the Eighteen Thirties on we find references to the "natural law" in numerous utterances of American economic writers as well as American businessmen and legislators. We hear about the "natural law" or the "economic law" or the "law of supply and demand" or the "laws of trade." And every dubious omission and commission of businessmen

was liable to be justified by the "natural law." When, for instance, in 1863 the New York state banks decided to fight the newly-established national banking system and refused to accept national bank notes on deposit, they justified such action by declaring that national bank notes would be subject to the "natural law of depreciation," so that they could not act differently.

In the era of the Robber Barons this way of thinking took a new turn. Accepting social Darwinism as their creed, businessmen came to believe that the survival of the fittest was the natural law which determined their actions, and consequently, they came to see their competitive struggles as essentially identical with the struggles for survival which take place in nature. As late as 1913 the manager of the New York Clearing House believed in social Darwinism and the president of the New York Stock Exchange stated before the Pujo Committee that self-preservation was the first "law of nature." Again it is obvious that there is no room for responsibility in such an atmosphere. . . .

Turning from fact to value judgments, we meet all too often a strange scale of values which is again due to business appearing to the average businessman as a purpose in itself while the rest of the world, the raison d'être for business, is considered a mere means. The . . . Money Trust Investigation of 1912 conducted by the Pujo Committee, provides some striking examples. The President of the New York Stock Exchange and large brokers could see nothing wrong in the wildest market manipulations and dubious practices which were actually forbidden later, in the Nineteen Thirties, when the Securities and Exchange Commission came into existence. But they considered it a hideous crime for a stock-exchange broker to split his commission. As the President of the New York Stock Exchange expressed it:

> The violation of the commission law we regard as one of the most infamous crimes that a man can commit against his fellow member in the stock exchange and as a gross breach of faith and wrong doing of the most serious nature and we consider it a crime that we should punish as severely as . . . the constitution permits. . . .

Besides developing a double standard of ethics on the basis of a warped judgment regarding the place of business in social life, businessmen also came to look at business and ethics as completely separate. One of the witnesses before the Pujo Committee answered a question with the statement: "You are asking me a moral question and I am answering you a Stock Exchange question." In this mental framework men themselves could gain a "market value." The author found the following passage in an unpublished letter by John Murray Forbes, the outstanding Boston merchant and financier, of May 3, 1847:

> There is a queer vague vein about the . . . blood which rather hurts them as men of business. They are amiable too and I have a general kind of family regard—but I am talking to you about their market value.

It would not be permissible to laugh off attitudes and unbalanced judgments such as have been cited in the preceding paragraphs. On the contrary, they are utterly dangerous, leading to self-destruction on the part of their holders. A passage from Plato's *Laws* may be quoted as bearing witness to this assertion:

> If one sins against the laws of proportion and gives something too big to something too small to carry it—too big sails to too small a ship, too big meals to too small a body, too big powers to too small a soul—the result is

bound to be a complete upset. In an outburst of *hybris* the overfed body . . . will rush into sickness, while the jack-in-office will rush into the unrighteousness that *hybris* always breeds.

If one agrees with Lord Keynes on the importance "for good or evil" of ideas of economics and political philosophers, one is bound to consider as of importance discrepancies due to a time lag between businessmen's thinking and the most advanced thinking of scholars. Comparison of both in various periods reveals that the businessman, and especially the American businessman, has always been several decades behind his time, his technical progressiveness notwithstanding.

The Wealth of Nations was published in 1776 and Ricardo's writings, which dealt the death blow to Mercantilism as a system of thought, were published in the Eighteen Tens. The American businessmen, as this author has found in his research and as Louis Hartz has shown recently, were Mercantilists at least as late as 1837, and some of them even by 1860. On the other hand, after 1870 when the belief in laissez-faire was declining in Europe, (in consequence of Cairnes's and Marshall's work in England or that of the historical school of economists in Germany, let alone the attacks of Marx and his disciples) the American businessmen became adherents to that creed without any reservation whatsoever: As a matter of fact, most of them have remained so up to this date, regardless of what is happening all over the world. . . .

Much more self-destructive, however, than weakness of businessmen has been their very efficiency and success, and in this connection the daimonic dominates the field and has full sway. Schumpeter, in his book *Capitalism, Socialism and Democracy,* has pointed to the fact and in most respects this author agrees with his analysis. But he wishes to put a different emphasis on various phenomena, necessary in this context, since Schumpeter looks at capitalism, while this author studies its standard bearer.

First of all, the tremendous success of certain businessmen due to creative achievements has led to an accumulation of power first in their hands and subsequently in that of business as such. This accumulation of power in turn forced those detrimentally affected thereby to grasp for power too, in order to withstand the pressure and to hold ground. Loyalty to the established system became for many people burdensome, because short-term advantages to be derived therefrom appeared out of proportion to the pressure.

Very rarely in history is it possible to see so clearly the beginning of a chain of events as in this case. At the time when big business was brought into existence and in consequence of this creative achievement that power accumulation took place of which we are speaking, the prevailing philosophy of government held by the majority of politicians and by the people at large was that of laissez-faire: the less government the better. Only in reaction to the increasing power of business leaders, underprivileged strata in America, such as were farmers at that time and labor, forced first the states and later the national government to assume protective functions. This implied government assuming more power than ever before in our history.

In the second instance, farmers and labor built up powerful organizations of their own. "Businessmen's activities," as Taylor rightly stressed, "have led to a collection of aggressive special interests, power groups (corporations, labor unions, farm organizations) the relations among which so nearly approach a state of war

as to keep us unsafely close to a forced choice between the extremely coercive state or chaos."

When one agrees that this chain of events is in the last analysis due to creative achievements of business leaders which *ipso facto* resulted in power, we face the clearest possible case of daimonic self-destruction, for in this warlike situation the businessman has already now lost relatively more power than farm groups or labor have gained. At least so it appears at this moment; and the downfall of the investment banker as the dominating force in our national economy is a case in point. . . .

Schumpeter, finally, has pointed out that there is no trace of mystic glamor about the business leader, which is what counts in the rule of men. Business leadership, as he correctly stressed, does not lead to leadership of nations, since "the ledger and the cost calculation absorb and confine" and do not develop those characteristics which the national leader requires. In America their traditional contempt for government until recently kept business leaders from seeking high and exacting public office. It is only necessary to compare the number of businessmen who became United States presidents with the number of soldiers who did so and their respective shares in the total population to see the point.

In the last analysis the accumulation of power did more harm than good to business. An aggravating element was the fact that control over the means of production which gave power was to a large extent absentee control (for example, the control by the investment banker). Moreover, it was and is the power of men who have only a comparatively small personal stake in the social structure concerned (the gigantic enterprises) from which they derive that power. This situation in turn easily leads to irresponsibility, which prevails in American business for historical and ideological reasons anyway. It is the scourge of American entrepreneurship.

To complete the picture, what has often been discussed must be repeated; namely, that concentration of power changed the structure of competition so as to make it what Professor Easterbrook has called "the competition of power aggregations." . . .

The author does not want to be misunderstood: he does not believe in the possibility or desirability of a restoration of "perfect" competition. He agrees with Schumpeter that monopolistic competition has real advantages for economic development.

But from the particular angle of this investigation he must stress the consequences of the disappearance of competition of the classical type: the specific stimulus which it had provided ceased to work. It is that stimulus which contributed so much to the success of the capitalistic business leader, a success which in turn led to that power accumulation which now proves to be a danger to the businessman's future. Thus a process of daimonic self-destruction began which can be characterized as classical. The phases are: competition, stimulation, exertion, achievement, success, large-scale enterprise.

At this point the daimonic comes into play [as shown in outline below].

A second trend toward daimonic self-destruction has been pointed out by Schumpeter too. He has correctly stressed that Gustav von Schmoller, the great Berlin economist, was aware of it as early as the first decade of this century. Schmoller expected that the development of large-scale enterprise, which can easily be considered the businessman's greatest organizational achievement, would lead to a bureaucratization which would make large-scale enterprise amenable to be taken over by government administrators. There is undoubtedly a strong trend in this direction.

More than twenty-five years ago, when a student at the University of Berlin, this author learned that the difference between business and government administration was flexibility versus rigidity. The former found expression in the balance sheet, the latter in the budget. If this was an analysis true for the time, the adoption of budgeting by business enterprises possesses historical significance as marking the point at which large-scale business and government administration began to converge. In America Jacob Schiff claimed the merit of having introduced budgeting into railroad practice in the Nineteen Hundreds.

So much is certain, that administrative flexibility which distinguished small and medium scale enterprise from government agencies was unavoidably lost with the development of those gigantic concerns to which we owe the present stream of goods and services.

Those large-scale business concerns

Large-Scale Enterprise

cut-throat competition		accumulation of power	
abandoning competition	competition of power aggregates	building of hostile power aggregates	
ceasing stimulus		relative loss of power	government control

must be managed on the basis of rules and regulations just as are government agencies. They work under the same organizational disadvantages which are reflected in what the public is prone to call "red tape." There is the same rigidity, the same "layering," the same difficulty for younger and lesser, though brilliant, employees to be seen, to have access to the man at the top, and to rise. Finally, to nepotism in the corporation corresponds patronage in the government agency.

There are, of course, still many highly dynamic industries which could not be efficiently managed by government administrators, but many enterprises, especially in the field of utilities, undoubtedly can. One could almost claim that in some fields the best ally of the businessman, especially of the irresponsible businessman, is today the irresponsible, if not corrupt, politician. The politician if incompetent as an officeholder and at the same time unwilling to abandon the age-old game of patronage and dubious self-aggrandizement is probably the worse of two evils.

The creative achievement of building large-scale enterprises has undermined the businessman's position for still another reason. If one calls "entrepreneur" the man or the men who alone or in common establish the purpose and the spirit of an enterprise, determine its major policies, and thus become responsible for its fate, one can readily see that in the modern large-scale concern entrepreneurial functions are fulfilled in co-operation by top executives and numerous employees way down the line.

They are thus fulfilled partly by real employees, not by quasi-employees, such as presidents and vice-presidents of corporations. The latter, unless they are men of genius, are just as small cogs in the machine, as are the men down the line who help to make up the team. The only difference may be that, located as they are at the top of the engine, they can be noticed. The chief executive co-ordinates, but the intrinsic value of those whom he co-ordinates will to a large extent determine his achievements. . . .

To sum up, the businessman's creative achievement of building large-scale industry, large-scale transportation enterprises, large-scale public utilities has brought into being conditions under which many of the carriers of the load in those enterprises are no longer vitally interested in their functioning as *free* (capitalistic) enterprises, that is to say, organizations handled by business leaders.

So far the analysis has paralleled Schumpeter's; at this point, however, we part company. One of the reasons why Schumpeter expects an ultimate breakdown of capitalism is the disappearance of innovation as a decisive function of business leaders. Innovation, according to Schumpeter, has become easier and easier, and finally a matter of organized routine. It has become amenable to team work and so the creative entrepreneur, highly remunerated for his achievements, who provided the capitalist class with ever new recruits, is disappearing. Through his achievements, so Schumpeter thinks, the creative entrepreneur has made himself superfluous.

With all due respect for Schumpeter, I think there are several flaws in his analysis. While the factual statements regarding team work and specialized activities in the field of innovation are undoubtedly correct, I do not think that far reaching innovation is becoming easier or will become so, that is to say, I do not see the daimonic in action just here. It is true that consumers' resistance to innovation has been broken down to a large extent and that it is comparatively easy to introduce minor innovations. But as for revolutionary innovations (and these are the ones which Schumpeter has in mind) it will be just as difficult as before, so the author believes, to introduce them into the practice. To be sure, resistance thereto will be located at different centers and the motives behind that resistance are becoming different from what they were in the past. In future resistance to revolutionary innovations will be located with the most powerful corporations, trade organizations, and labor unions, and there will be extraordinary resistance to innovation *within* gigantic enterprises when it means writing off scores or hundreds of millions of capital. The creative entrepreneur of the future, presumably a corporation official, will have to overcome first of all formidable resistance in his own enterprise, and he will probably have to be a diplomat rather than a salesman or advertiser. . . .

Even if one disagrees with Schumpeter on the question of whether the success of the innovating business leader has led to daimonic self-destruction by making innovation teachable routine, the existence of daimonic self-destructiveness of business leaders should now be clear beyond a doubt. In the end daimonic destructiveness and daimonic self-destructiveness have merged to form a tragic concatenation. Of course the modern business leader is the descendant of medieval merchants who were part and parcel of Western civilization. But when in the eighteenth and nineteenth centuries the creative, the innovating, business leader appeared in comparatively large numbers he began by his very achievement to undermine the European civilization and he helped to bring it to the brink of that collapse where it now

stands. Schumpeter touched upon the problem when he discussed the destruction of those strata which had protected the business leader in the era of early and in the first decades of high capitalism. But one must go much further. This author thinks that he cannot make the point clearer than by using Toynbee's words:

> The introduction of any new dynamic forces or creative movements into the life of a society ought to be accompanied by a reconstruction of the whole existing set of institutions if a healthy harmony is to be preserved.

Otherwise it is followed by disintegration, due to

> disharmony between the institutions of which a society is composed . . . [and the] new social forces . . . which the existing set of institutions was not originally designed to carry.

This is exactly what has happened to Western Civilization when the creative business leader began revolutionizing it. There was no reconstruction, there was just daimonic destruction to make room for building a productive apparatus such as the world has never before seen. The revolutionary forces represented by the creative business leader could not be absorbed because of the speed alone with which the creative-destructive process took place. . . . Or to put it differently, in the process of daimonic destructiveness the business leader is destroying the civilization to which he belongs and thereby the soil in which he roots. Thus in the last act of the tragedy daimonic destructiveness has turned daimonic self-destructiveness and this is what was meant when the author spoke earlier of a concatenation of daimonic destructiveness and daimonic self-destructiveness.

Here it is necessary, however, to distinguish between European and American conditions. So far, America has been and is part and parcel of Western civilization, but it may be on the point of parting company from it. The amorphousness of American society, the absence of a proletariat as Europe has it and of a proletariat in the sense of Toynbee, and finally various other social phenomena may be indicative of that trend which, if it exists at all, must be in a very early stage. If, as seems possible, the next few hundred years should experience the emergence of a genuine American civilization *(Kulturkreis)* affiliated to the Western, modern business may well appear as one of its basic institutions and the creative business leader may, *sub specie aeternitatis,* have been among those who laid the cornerstone of the new civilization. To a large extent that will depend on the wisdom of the American businessmen as a class, to repeat: wisdom and not technical skill, but one cannot see very much of that.

To sum up: in the opinion of the author by a daimonic process of destruction and self-destruction the *ruggedly individualistic and socially irresponsible* businessman of the nineteenth century has doomed himself, not because of his weakness or wickedness, but *because of his creative achievements* for our material civilization. *Because* of his achievements he is becoming an archaic type. What is now needed is a creative achievement of first magnitude, but one of a character entirely different from the business leaders' creative achievements of the past: the type "businessman" must be reshaped so as to fit into a coming economic order (style) which will be as different from that prevailing in the nineteenth century as it should be, so at least we hope, different from that of communism. But in order to make room for that achievement the leading businessmen must reorient their thinking. They had better forget Adam Smith, John Stuart Mill, invisible hand, and natural law, and look at the world without out-of-date theorizing. They need that humility of which Donald K. David speaks. What the businessman has experienced in the last few decades is the nemesis of creativity. Another act of creation is necessary if he is to have a new lease of life, that is to say, if he wants to be permitted to contribute what he actually has to offer.

Suggestions for Further Reading

The Gilded Age businessman has served as subject for many more writers than those noted in this volume. The only bibliographical essay that attempts to cover the entire historical growth of the robber baron controversy is Hal Bridges, "The Robber Baron Concept in American History," *Business History Review*, XXXII (Spring, 1958), pp. 1–13. As the title implies, David Chalmers, "From Robber Barons to Industrial Statesmen: Standard Oil and the Business Historians," *American Journal of Economics and Sociology*, XX (October, 1960), pp. 47–58, deals with one company. Edward Chase Kirkland, in "The Robber Barons Revisited," *American Historical Review*, LXVI (October, 1960), pp. 68–73, reviews recent revisionist writings but remains pessimistic about their success in changing academicians' minds. A more complete but not carefully annotated listing may be found in Kirkland's biographical notes in his *Industry Comes of Age: Business, Labor, and Public Policy, 1860–1897* (New York, 1961), pp. 410–436. Robert H. Walker surveys the mogul in one form of literature in "The Poet and the Robber Baron," *American Quarterly*, XIX (Winter, 1961), pp. 447–465.

William Woodruff criticizes both the muckrakers and the revisionists in "History and the Businessman," *Business History Review*, XXX (September, 1956), pp. 241–259, but offers no workable alternative. Allen Solganick proves that the Josephson school remains very much alive in "The Robber Baron Concept and Its Revisionists," *Science and Society*, XXIX (Summer, 1965), pp. 257–269. See also Gabriel Kolko's perceptive "The Premises of Business Revisionism," *Business History Review*, XXXIII (1959), pp. 330–344, which points out the similarities in style between the revisionists and Marxist theoreticians. Matthew Josephson and Allan Nevins debate the merits and faults of both positions in "Should American History Be Rewritten?" *Saturday Review of Literature*, XXXVII (February 6, 1954), 7–10; 44–49.

Few surveys of the post-Civil War era exist, compared with the number of works on all or part of the twentieth century. Of recent efforts, H. Wayne Morgan, ed., *The Gilded Age: A Reappraisal* (Syracuse, N.Y., 1963) attempts to reinterpret the period but accomplishes its goal with only varying degrees of success. In *Age of Excess: The United States from 1877 to 1914* (New York, 1965), Ray Ginger finds almost nothing but villains, while Bernard A. Weisberger fluctuates between muckraker and revisionist in *The New Industrial Society* (New York, 1969). Carl N. Degler, *The Age of Economic Revolution, 1876–1900* (Glenview, Ill., 1967) and John A. Garraty, *The New Commonwealth, 1877–1890* (New York, 1968) both acknowledge and incorporate recent studies and are the most objective books on the period.

The origin of the term robber baron is obscure, but E. L. Godkin, editor of *The Nation*, applied it in "The Vanderbilt Memorial," *The Nation*, IX (November 18, 1869), pp. 431–432. Charles Francis Adams cited its use by the Grangers in *Railroads: Their Origin and Problems* (New York, 1893). The term caught on and spread rapidly in the early twentieth century. The familiarity of mid-century Americans with the term dates from Matthew Josephson, *The Robber Barons: The Great American Capitalists, 1861–1901* (New York, 1934).

The picture of the businessman as a robber baron was first painted by late-nineteenth-century writers such as Charles Francis Adams, Jr., *Chapters of Erie and Other Essays* (New York, 1886) and Henry Demarest Lloyd, *Wealth Against Commonwealth* (New York,

1894). Chester McArthur Destler upholds Lloyd's accuracy in "Wealth Against Commonwealth, 1894 and 1944," *American Historical Review,* XL (April, 1944), pp. 49–69, while Allan Nevins dissents in a letter published in vol. L (April, 1945), pp. 676–689. Destler continues his defense in *Henry Demarest Lloyd and the Empire of Reform* (Philadelphia, 1963). John Tipple claims that the failure to recognize new problems led to the attack on the moguls in "The Anatomy of Prejudice: Origins of the Robber Baron Legend," *Business History Review,* XXXIII (Winter, 1959), pp. 510–523.

A few entrepreneurs recorded their view of the Gilded Age in later years. Andrew Carnegie, *Autobiography* (Boston, 1920) and *The Gospel of Wealth and Other Timely Essays* (New York, 1900), Henry Villard, *Memoirs . . . [a] Journalist and Financier,* (2 vols.; Boston, 1904), and John D. Rockefeller, *Random Reminicences of Men and Events* (New York, 1909) represent efforts by the moguls to explain their actions. The many government hearings and investigations conducted in the period, such as the five volumes of the U.S. Pacific Railway Commission (1887) and the U.S. Industrial Commission Report on Trusts (1800 1000), are valuable as research tools.

During the Progressive era of the early twentieth century men strove to correct many of the nation's problems, among which the abuse of corporate power and the inequalities of wealth ranked high. As a result, many writers turned their guns on the businessman as the archvillain of society. Theodore Roosevelt dubbed this group of writers and journalists the muckrakers, perhaps a tribute to their effective influencing of public attitudes toward the business leader. In *Sin and Society: An Analysis of Latter-day Iniquity* (New York, 1907), Edward A. Ross attacked corporate morals; Upton Sinclair exposed the dismal working conditions in the meat-packing industry in *The Jungle* (New York, 1906); Lincoln Steffens condemned the relationship between politics and business in *The Shame of the Cities* (New York, 1904); and Ida M. Tarbell continued Lloyd's attack on John D.

Rockefeller in *The History of the Standard Oil Company* (New York, 1904). Articles in magazines such as *Cosmopolitan, Collier's, New Republic, Atlantic Monthly, McClure's, Forum,* and *American Magazine* influenced public thinking more than books, perhaps because of their wider circulation. Although old, C. C. Regier, *The Era of the Muckrakers* (Chapel Hill, N.C., 1932) remains one of the best summaries of this journalism; but see also Daniel Aaron, *Men of Good Hope* (New York, 1951). Because Thorstein Veblen influenced the climate of opinion toward social legislation, the student must not overlook his two classics, *The Theory of the Leisure Class* (New York, 1899) and *The Theory of Business Enterprise* (New York, 1904).

During the 1920s public sentiment became more favorable to business than it had ever been before. Yet two historians of the Progressive tradition aided in keeping the robber baron interpretation alive. Charles A. Beard, in his and Mary Beard's *The Rise of American Civilization* (2 vols.; New York, 1927), acknowledges some positive contributions of the businessman, but still categorizes him as a robber baron. Vernon L. Parrington recognizes no virtue in the entrepreneur; the only restraining element on the virulence in his *Main Currents in American Thought* (3 vols.; New York, 1927–1930) is the limitation of the English language.

While the academicians continued to write in robber baron terms, journalists of the 1920s turned out a series of highly laudatory biographies written to influence public opinion. Some of these, such as George B. M. Harvey, *Henry Clay Frick, The Man* (New York, 1928) and E. D. McCafferty, *Henry J. Heinz, A Biography* (New York, 1925), treat the businessman with such lack of scholarly objectivity that they are rejected by both the robber baron writers and revisionist historians. However, such works should not be ignored as they represent a popular approach during the decade.

As the United States suffered through the grave economic crisis of the 1930s, an intensified attack on big business developed in various books and journals. The student must understand the deep frustrations of the American people in seeing the nation's economic foundations crack, particularly after they had been convinced in the 1920s of the business-man's stewardship of the country. These feelings are clearly described in Harvey Swados, ed., *The American Writer and the Great Depression* (Indianapolis, 1966), Daniel Aaron, *Writers on the Left* (New York, 1961), and John Dos Passos, *U.S.A.* (3 vols.; Boston, 1930, 1932, 1936). The most influential book of the period on the captains of industry, a work that continues to be assigned reading in many courses, is Matthew Josephson, *The Robber Barons*. Based to a large extent on Gustavus Myers, *History of the Great American Fortunes* (New York, 1910), it reflects much of the Marxist tone common in the 1930s. Allan Nevins disagrees with Josephson's thesis in a review that appeared in The *Saturday Review of Literature*, X (March 3, 1934), p. 522.

Despite an overwhelming antibusiness bias among writers, the portent of a changing attitude could be detected during the 1930s. A few writers, such as Burton J. Hendrick, *The Life of Andrew Carnegie* (2 vols.; Garden City, N.Y., 1932), continued the almost reverent approach of the 1920s. Others approached their subject more objectively and after much historical research; Allan Nevins, *Abram S. Hewitt: With Some Account of Peter Cooper* (New York, 1935) and Henrietta M. Larson, *Jay Cooke: Private Banker* (Cambridge, Mass., 1936) are leading examples. This group began countering the robber baron interpretation with the idea of the "creative capitalist," a theme developed more extensively in the two succeeding decades.

After 1940, with the return of prosperity and a more conservative political climate as well as more dispassionate writers, the trend of American historiography slowly retreated from the socially oriented robber baron approach and moved toward a better balanced economic view of the Gilded Age entrepreneur and his work. In 1940 Allan Nevins reevaluated earlier accounts of the Standard Oil Company in *John D. Rockefeller: The Heroic Age of American Enterprise,* in which he emphasized the oil mogul's constructive accomplishments. Thirteen years later, after the discovery

of new material, Nevins reiterated this position in *Study in Power: John D. Rockefeller, Industrialist and Philanthropist* (2 vols.; New York, 1953).

In a paper presented at a meeting of the American Historical Association, entitled "The Social Role of the Corporation," Thomas C. Cochran emphasized the need for historical research in determining the relationship of business to social development. It was later published in Caroline F. Ware, ed., *The Cultural Approach to History* (Port Washington, N.Y., 1940). In 1942 Cochran coauthored with William Miller, *The Age of Enterprise: A Social History of Industrial America* (New York, 1942), which views the business leader as both shaping and responding to the country's value system. Louis Hacker, a former Marxist, stresses the moguls' creative abilities in his *Triumph of American Capitalism* (New York, 1940), and continues this theme in *The World of Andrew Carnegie* (Philadelphia, 1967), which analyzes the period more than Carnegie.

In 1948 reevaluation of the businessman and society led to the creation of a Research Center in Entrepreneurial History at Harvard. Its activities resulted in several major contributions. In *Railroad Leaders, 1845–1890: The Business Mind in Action* (New York, 1953), Thomas C. Cochran found sixty-one railroad executives to be conservative, but he rejects the robber baron label. Sigmund Diamond examined the obituaries of late-nineteenth-century businessmen and discovered little evidence of public disfavor, as reported in *The Reputation of the American Businessman* (Cambridge, Mass., 1955). Harold Passer, in *The Electrical Manufacturers, 1875–1900* (Cambridge, Mass., 1953), focuses on entrepreneurial innovations in that industry and brilliantly synthesizes their creative and destructive impacts.

Another group of historians refuse to accept the name revisionist, although the term fits their objectives. Less interested in the businessman's social conduct than in the efficient internal administration of the firm, they basically reject the robber baron attack on the businessman's social responsibility. Developed from the efforts of N. S. B. Gras of Harvard, those who use this approach are identified as the Harvard Group. The publications using this frame of reference, such as Ralph W. and Muriel Hidy, *Pioneering in Big Business, 1882–1911* (New York, 1955), vol. I of the *History of the Standard Oil Company,* and Ralph W. Hidy, Frank Hill, and Allan Nevins, *Timber and Men: The Weyerhauser Story* (New York, 1963), judge the businessman on his ability to manage a successful corporation. As firms often subsidize a history, the possibility of management influence on content disturbs some scholars, such as John K. Galbraith in "Even Their Best Friends Won't Tell Them," *The Reporter,* XVI (1954), pp. 39–42.

Besides the organized groups mentioned above, many other writers since World War II have provided better insight into Gilded Age business. Edward C. Kirkland stands out as the leading revisionist, with several studies, all sympathetic to the businessmen and emphasizing his constructive contributions. In addition to *Dream and Thought in the Business Community, 1860–1900* (Ithaca, N.Y., 1956), he has written *Business in the Gilded Age: The Conservatives' Balance Sheet* (Madison, Wis., 1952) and *Industry Comes of Age: Business, Labor and Public Policy, 1860 1897* (New York, 1961). Julius Grodinsky exceeds even Kirkland when he praises the railroad capital and construction contributions of one of the era's archvillains in *Jay Gould: His Business Career, 1867–1892* (Philadelphia, 1957). Jonathan R. Hughes stresses the creative abilities of Vanderbilt and Morgan in *The Vital Few: American Economic Progress and Its Protagonists* (Boston, 1966), and Davis P. Gagan defends another railroad leader in "The Railroads and the Public, 1870–1881; A Study of Charles Elliot Perkins' Business Ethics," *Business History Review,* XXXIX (Spring, 1965), pp. 41–56. A popular account by journalist Steward Holbrook, *The Age of the Moguls* (New York, 1953), anecdotal and unanalytical, leaves no doubt of its admiration of the businessman. An open defense of the captains of industry also forms the base of *The Enterprising Americans* (New York, 1963), written by the *Wall Street Journal*'s John Chamberlain.

A few historians continue to resist the trend toward a softening of the robber baron interpretation. Chester McArthur Destler upholds the older view in a number of works including "Standard Oil, Child of the Erie Ring," *Mississippi Valley Historical Review,* XXXIII (1945), pp. 89–114; *American Radicalism, 1865–1901* (New York, 1946); "Opposition of American Businessmen to Social Control During the 'Gilded Age,'" *Mississippi Valley Historical Review,* XXXIX (1953), pp. 641–672; and *Roger Sherman and the Independent Oil Men* (Ithaca, N.Y., 1967). John Tipple is not asking a question but answering it in "The Robber Baron in the Gilded Age: Entrepreneur or Iconoclast?" in Morgan, ed., *The Gilded Age: A Reappraisal* (Syracuse, N.Y., 1963). Sometimes the title indicates the author's position, as in Sidney I. Roberts, "Portrait of a Robber Baron: Charles T. Yerkes," *Business History Review,* XXXV (Autumn, 1961), pp. 344–371.

Writings on the other specific issues raised in the present volume have not been as extensive as those assessing the mogul's motives and methods. The small amount of work on Social Darwinism tends to follow the Hofstadter approach. This may be detected in works like Bert Loewenberg, "Darwinism Comes to America, 1859–1900," *Mississippi Valley Historical Review,* XXVIII (December, 1941), and the chapters in Stow Persons, ed., *Evolutionary Thought in America* (New Haven, Conn., 1950) and Philip P. Wiener, *Evolution and the Founders of Pragmatism* (Cambridge, Mass., 1949). Evidences of Wyllie's criticism appear in Cochran, *Railroad Leaders* and Kirkland, *Dream and Thought in the Business Community.*

Many late-nineteenth-century Americans, as well as many today, believed the Horatio Alger rags-to-riches development of the Gilded Age entrepreneur. Recent studies, notably Irvin G. Wyllie, *The Self-Made Man in America* (New York, 1954), refute this position. In his *Apostles of the Self-Made Man* (Chicago, 1965), John G. Cawelti traces the growth of the concept, while Francis W. Gregory and Irene D. Neu shed further light on the moguls' privileged backgrounds in "The American Industrial Elite in the 1870s: Their Social Origins," in William Miller, ed., *Men in Business* (Cambridge, Mass., 1952).

For some of the best sources on the Gilded Age value system, consult the contemporary magazines: *Harper's, North American Review, Atlantic Monthly,* and *Scribner's.* Two general surveys of the cultural and artistic life of the era, Thomas Beer, *The Mauve Decade: American Life at the End of the Nineteenth Century* (New York, 1926) and Lewis Mumford, *The Brown Decades* (New York, 1931) are rather critical. The Crassness of the period dominated the interpretation of Vernon L. Parrington (already cited) and set the tone of later writers. Recently, however, some voices have rejected this stereotyped view. Such a demurrer is Robert R. Roberts, "Gilt, Gingerbread, and Realism: The Public and Its Taste," in Morgan, ed., *The Gilded Age: A Reappraisal.*

Most writing on labor concentrates on union organization, with bad working conditions either taken for granted or disposed of in one or two pages. *Transactions of the American Society of Mechanical Engineers,* which began in 1880, is an excellent contemporary source on the worker's problems. Virtually all the studies on strikes and organization, such as John R. Commons, et. al., *History of Labour in the United States* (4 vols.; New York, 1918–1935) or the newer, well-respected volume by Lloyd Ulman, *The Rise of the National Trade Union* (Cambridge, Mass., 1955) accept the robber baron theme. Kirkland, in his discussion of labor conditions in *Industry Comes of Age,* softens some of the criticism, while Herbert Gutman expands the thesis presented in this volume in "Class, Status and Community Power in Nineteenth Century American In-

dustrial Cities—Paterson, New Jersey: A Case Study," in Frederic C. Jaher, ed., *The Age of Industrialism in America: Essays in Social Structure and Cultural Values* (New York, 1968). Charles N. Glaab and Lawrence H. Larsen find Gutman's position untenable with respect to a small Wisconsin community portrayed in *Factories in the Valley: Neenah-Menasha, 1870–1910* (Madison, Wis., 1968).

Virtually all writing on the moguls and politics reflects the Myers' position in this volume. Matthew Josephson leaned heavily on Myers for his *Robber Barons* and injects the same view in *The Politicos, 1865–1896* (New York, 1938). Even in a so-called revisionist work—Morgan, ed., *The Gilded Age: A Reappraisal*—Vincent P. DeSantis, in "The Republican Party Revisited, 1877–1897," accepts the standard business-political alliance. Rothman advanced relatively new ideas in his *Politics and Power: The United States Senate, 1869–1901* (Cambridge, Mass., 1966), from which a selection is reprinted in the present volume. Cochran and Miller in *The Age of Enterprise* establish stages in the development of political control but concede its dominance by the 1880s. Several recent works demonstrate that a homogeneous "business community" did not exist and that businessmen often worked at cross-purposes in the political arena. Excellent examples are Robert P. Sharkey, *Money, Class, and Party: An Economic Study of the Civil War and Reconstruction* (Baltimore, Md., 1959); Stanley Coben, "Northeastern Business and Radical Reconstruction: A Re-examination," *Mississippi Valley Historical Review,* XLVI (1959); and Lee Benson, *Merchants, Farmers, and Railroads: Railroad Regulation and New York Politics, 1850–1887* (Cambridge, Mass., 1955).